Social Skills for Teens With Social Anxiety

Manage Anxiety, Avoid Awkwardness, Feel Comfortable in Any Social Situations, and Make Real Friends

Grace Cohen

Contents

Bonus Ebook (Scan the QR code below)

https://dl.bookfunnel.com/s3hiwut9vr

Introduction

If you are reading this book, then it is very likely that you are a teenager that struggles with social anxiety. Many teenagers today struggle with social anxiety, also known as social phobia. This makes teens like you constantly worry about what others think of you and of how you will act according to the social situation you are in. Social phobia can significantly deteriorate the quality of your life by making it difficult for you to speak, engage in sports or any other extracurricular activity, or do a variety of different things that require that you interact with others. You may also have a hard time at school since social phobia can make it hard for you to form friendships and become a part of a group.

It is important for you to know that your condition is not isolated and that you are not alone in this fight. There has been a study that researched how common social anxiety is among young people in seven different countries (Russia, Brazil, China, United States, Thailand, Vietnam, and Indonesia) and the results indicate that social phobia is actually rather common among youth. A survey that used the Social Interaction Anxiety Scale (SIAS) looked at the data from 6,825 participants, and of those participants 1 in 3 qualified as having Social Anxiety Disorder (SAD). This amounts to 36% of participants having social anxiety.

How severe and prevalent the anxiety was, did not change among genders but did vary based on the young person's age, work status, country, education level, and whether they were in a rural or urban area. It is also interesting to note that 1 in 6 viewed themselves as not suffering from SAD but still met the criteria of the disorder. What this study demonstrates is that many young people across the globe face social anxiety issues, but unfortunately there are those among that population that deny their struggles. The number of young people that also had impairments in their well-being and functioning was also large (Jefferies & Ungar, 2020).

Another study with a research population of 210 research subjects found other results that may reassure you that you are not alone. Social anxiety has its onset (meaning the time in which the disorder starts) in the early to mid-teen years of individuals, and most people with Social Anxiety Disorder will have gotten it before they turn 20 years old. This means that teenagers like you are particularly prone to experiencing social anxiety since the symptoms usually begin around adolescence. Social anxiety is the third leading mental health disorder in the United States, with depression and alcohol use disorder before it (National Collaborating Centre for Mental Health, 2013).

Life is already complicated and hard enough as it is, and so adding on social anxiety is an extra hurdle to overcome. Having a social phobia can make your life seem like a living hell of some sorts at times since it greatly diminishes your confidence in your social abilities, isolates you from personal and career opportunities that can make you grow, makes you have a very low opinion of yourself, and keeps you away from making deep and meaningful connections with others. It becomes even harder to cope with the negative effects of social anxiety when you consider your age group. Adolescence is often a very tumultuous time since it is a period of your life in which you are discovering your self-identity and getting a sense of who you are as a student, as a friend, as a family member, and as a member of your community. It may seem like you have a lot on your plate when you add on external stressors that often take place in adolescence such as bullying, peer pressure, drugs and alcohol, sexual activity, and rigorous classes. Thus, social anxiety and adolescence seem to be a recipe for disaster.

The Solution to This Problem

The good news is that social anxiety can be treated with adequate and necessary interventions and psychoeducation. In other words, there is hope for you! You can still live a happy and fulfilling teenage life despite your social anxiety. This book thus strives to serve as a beacon of hope for every single teenager out there that is struggling with social anxiety. These pages will be an excellent resource for teens like you that are dealing with social phobia and have a hard time with social skills. This book will teach you to feel more at ease when you are in social situations through a wide array of different techniques, exercises, and strategies. I will also teach you how to make the most out of the time you have by guiding you through the process of conquering and defeating social anxiety. I will also be teaching you valuable social skills that will not only be useful in your teenage life but will also help you as you grow into adulthood, enter the workforce, and/or go to college.

Before you go on reading, I want to express that I know how you may or may not be thinking. There is a good chance that you may have gotten this book from your worried parents, or perhaps from another well-meaning family member or even a therapist. You may think that self-help books are overrated and boring, or that you have nothing to learn from this book. It is not uncommon for teenagers to dread "grown-up things" such as self-help guides and books, and so I understand that you may be skeptical, especially if you did not buy this book yourself. However, please give me a chance to show you that the strategies listed in this book are effective. Who knows who you may be by the time you finish this book? You could transform from a shy and socially anxious teenager into one that is full of confidence and knows how to successfully interact with others without invoking their social phobia. After all, you have nothing to lose by reading this book and every single possibility of learning to thrive and flourish through the wisdom that I will pass on to you.

The first chapter will go into detail about what social anxiety is and how to know if you have it since knowing your enemy is the first step you need to take to defeat it. Chapter 2 will then talk about the social skills that you need as a teen and why they are so important. Chapter 3 will go into the details of Cognitive Behavioral Therapy (CBT), which is a standard intervention that is used to treat Social Anxiety Disorder, and Chapter 4 will go into the details of Dialectical Behavioral Therapy (DBT), another standard intervention that is used to treat SAD. In these two chapters, I will talk about what CBT and DBT therapy are like and what you can expect from them, as well as give you helpful techniques from these treatments that you can use whether you have a therapist or not. Chapter 5 will elaborate on the social skills that I listed in Chapter 2 and will give you strategies to enhance your social skills. Chapter 6 is all about overcoming social anxiety through other techniques that are outside of CBT and DBT. Lastly, Chapter 7 will teach you how to boost your confidence in yourself and show you how you can become the best version of yourself. I will also leave you with a conclusion that will summarize the most important key points that you have learned.

I also want to mention the fact that this book is not a substitute for a mental health provider and that you should not use it as such. As a matter of fact, I encourage you to work with your therapist as you keep reading this book so that you can work with them through the exercises I provide. This book is meant to guide you through defeating social anxiety and gaining social skills, but it cannot provide direct psychiatric or psychological treatment. Keep in mind that there are certain exercises in this book that may be difficult for you to complete (especially the exposure-based ones), which is why I recommend that you reach out to your parents and therapist (if you have one) if you are in a mental health crisis.

The Credibility of This Book

CBT and DBT, two of the treatments that I will be talking about, are usually regarded as the golden standard in psychology. This is because these interventions are heavily evidence-based and have an extensive research literature that backs them up. For instance, in a study that used CBT to treat Social Anxiety Disorder, it was found that just six brief weekly CBT therapies were effective in decreasing the patients' social anxiety. It was found that patients that took these CBT sessions improved in a way that was clinically significant (Sudhir et al., 2015). DBT has also been shown to be more effective in treating anxiety than other treatments (Harned & Botanov, 2016). I have also gathered information concerning social skills and other forms of social anxiety treatment through reputable, trustworthy, and accredited sources such as the American Psychological Association, Verywell Mind, the National Library of Medicine, Dr. Gail Gross, Mayo Clinic, Psychology Today, University Hospitals, and also peer-reviewed journals such as PLOS ONE, Cognitive Therapy and Research, and Psychiatric Times.

On top of this, I am the mother of two sons. I had to learn how to parent my children and foster social skills in them, and my journey has given me valuable experience on the struggles teenagers face that can lead to them experiencing social anxiety. As you may imagine, my sons and I had to do a lot of hard work to get them to a point in which they were confident in their social abilities since adolescence is a very hard time for all teens. Teaching my children how to develop their social skills was a part of my journey that is very dear to me, and one that I want to share by giving teenagers like you the resources I gave to my sons so they could thrive and grow as sociable human beings.

The Benefits of Reading This Book

Reading this book can quite literally change your life for the better. I will teach you invaluable skills that can help you lessen your social anxiety and better your social skills. I have already explained to you that CBT and DBT are clinically significant and effective treatments for social anxiety and anxiety overall, which is proof that the strategies that I will teach you in this book will work. In addition, I know that social skills are an invaluable part of life that every human should get to expand and develop, and reading this book will benefit you by teaching you how to develop these social skills. This can benefit your relationships with your family, friends, and teachers. I also want to stress that improving your social skills, in the long run, can greatly increase your chances of success in the workforce and higher education should you choose to pursue it. Don't believe me? The proof is evident when you think about the fact that many colleges and universities will ask for letters of recommendation when you are applying to study in them, and many jobs will ask you for professional references when you are applying to them. By learning the social skills in this book, you will be able to better relate with your teachers, coworkers, and supervisors, all of which can provide you with these letters of recommendation and/or job references.

Take a Stance in Your Social Life by Reading This Book

This book promises to significantly improve your life by helping you overcome social anxiety and by giving you valuable social skills tools. It is critical and urgent that you read this book if you have social anxiety so that you can take your life back and be the teenager you are meant to be. So go on, keep reading this book! I will be with you every single step of the way. However, in order for this to work you need to keep your side of the promise by reading this book carefully. I will hold true to my promise and guide you toward the teenage life you have been looking for.

Chapter 1

Do You Have Social Anxiety?

How does it feel to have social anxiety? This may seem like a loaded question, and that is because it absolutely is. There is no single universal social anxiety experience, but there are many commonalities among people that struggle with Social Anxiety Disorder. However, for the sake of this question let's think of this question in a picture format.

Having social anxiety is like having a black hole deep within your heart that drains you of the ability to interact with others, which is why you may avoid these social situations like the plague. Little do you know that by avoiding your very same fear all you are doing is feeding the black hole in your heart and allowing it to take control of you until you withdraw from people, places, and events that can give you joy. Social anxiety is sitting alone at lunch because you cannot bring yourself to ask the other kids at the school if you can sit at their table no matter how much you want to. For the black hole gnaws at you and blatantly disregards your desire for social companionship, and instead consumes that very wish and leaves you empty.

Having social anxiety is like looking at a haunted mirror that tells you the most wicked things about yourself and distorts the way you look. Instead of looking at your face, the mirror shows you a monster, a horrendous version of yourself that depicts your every weakness with a cruel paintbrush, just like Dorian Gray's picture. Little do you know that the monster staring back at you does not even exist to begin with! It is but a false creation of the mirror that is meant to enslave you to it. Social anxiety is purposefully avoiding a classmate outside of school because how could they look at what you see in the haunted mirror and feel nothing but disgust?

Having social anxiety is like a bee that stings you over and over again, except this is no common bee. With every sting, it injects a poison that makes you doubt every single one of your abilities and it also drains you of every drop of confidence in your body. This gluttonous bee sucks the joy away from you and keeps it all for itself. Little do you know that this bee is powerless against you and that you could swat it away with the right tools. Social anxiety is having a nervous breakdown during your history presentation because the bee has stung you so many times that all it has left you with is an overwhelming sense of self-doubt and insecurity.

Having social anxiety is like having an invisibility cloak on you, except unlike Harry Potter you think you cannot take the invisibility cloak off. The cloak makes it seem as though you were a wallflower, for it disconnects you from everyone around you, yet you think it is there to protect you. After all, without it, you would be bare and exposed to the social situations that you fear so much, and so your invisibility cloak is sewn with the yarn of avoidance. Little do you know that that cloak is actually hindering you instead of protecting you and that if you build your own wand you can yell, *"Expecto Patronum!"* and have your Patronus take it off for you. Social anxiety is running in the opposite direction when you see that a person you know is saying hi to you, for the cloak has convinced you that it will keep you safe from the dangers of unexpected social encounters like this one.

What Is Social Anxiety Disorder? (Social Phobia)

Humans are intrinsically social beings, and having social connections with other people is essential to their mental and physical welfare. If you lack social skills or connections, you can isolate yourself and even fail to grow and thrive as an individual. Ask yourself the following questions as a way to get started on acknowledging that you have social anxiety:

- Have you always been "shy" and struggled to socially interact and mix with other people?

-

Have you realized that you have a hard time in social situations?

- Is this something that has been building up throughout your teenage years and has also been influenced by world events such as the Covid-19 pandemic?

Social Anxiety Disorder (SAD), also known as social phobia, is a mental health condition that consists of a strong and continuous fear of embarrassment, judgment, rejection, or scrutiny from others. SAD is a mental health condition that is recognized by the Diagnostic and Statistical Manual of Mental Disorders. People with this disorder usually have strong beliefs that tell them that other people will criticize and/or negatively judge them in social situations. Social anxiety can be rather intense and can affect every single aspect of your life as a teenager. SAD can make teenagers struggle when it comes to maintaining their relationships, and thus also leads to plummeting in these relationships. Social anxiety also increases isolation and withdrawal and can complicate mental health problems. This is especially true right now due to the Covid-19 pandemic since this major world event created an interruption in the social development of teenagers. Social phobia cases have taken a sharp increase over the last few years precisely because of the pandemic.

There are many areas in which you as a teenager can experience social anxiety, such as:

-

During performance scenarios (such as public speaking or presenting information to others)

- In any physical problems that are difficult to talk about or that limit you

- Attending social meetings, parties, or situations that are new

- The beginning of a romantic partnership

- Drinking or eating in public

- Making new acquaintances or meeting strangers (Russell, 2022)

SAD is a diverse condition and not a monolith at all since some people with social anxiety may be scared of only one or two social situations while others can suffer from social anxiety in many or nearly all social situations. As you already know from the introduction, social anxiety usually surfaces during adolescence. According to the National Institute of Mental Health (NIMH), SAD takes place among 12% of shy teenagers, and these teenagers are usually around the age of 13. Most teenagers like you may encounter normal anxiety levels as they progress through adolescence, but teenagers with SAD have anxiety and fear that is disproportionate to the situations that they are in. During adolescence, there are many brain changes that help you become more socially aware, and your peer group as a teenager can be of uttermost importance. Thus, these facts may be why SAD is common among teenagers (Guy-Evans, 2022).

What Causes Social Anxiety in Teens?

There is no single factor that solely causes SAD, but there are many different factors such as brain chemistry, environmental factors, genetics, and so on. Here are some common factors that are said to cause SAD in teenagers:

Personality

There are certain types of personalities that are more prone to experiencing SAD. Children that have a quiet temperament may have a heightened risk of experiencing SAD when they start to become teenagers. Withdrawn children and children that are unwilling to try new things are also more likely to develop SAD in adolescence.

Parenting Style

Experts believe that parenting styles could be associated with the development of social anxiety in teenagers. Specifically, "helicopter parents" (also known as overprotective parents) are thought to make their children more prone to SAD. Overprotective parents often prevent their children from obtaining healthy social interaction levels, and they may also stop them from taking on risks. Thus, children and teenagers with overprotective parents will often have been deprived of the chance to learn coping skills that they will need in some circumstances.

Bullying

Bullying is rampant among children and teenagers, and this bullying can take place in online spaces or at school. Bullying often makes its victims fear social situations, and this can contribute to SAD. Being a victim of bullying may decrease someone's confidence and affect many areas of their life, which can lead to the development of social anxiety.

Environmental Factors

Social anxiety can arise as a defense mechanism toward social situations if someone is placed in an extremely embarrassing situation. Humans can learn to be anxious and tie this anxiety to an event or stimuli, such as opening up to people. If you had a traumatic experience, (or multiple traumatic experiences) you may develop maladaptive coping mechanisms since humans learn to cope in their environments. An example of a maladaptive coping mechanism that is present in SAD is believing that never interacting with anyone is the best way to avoid being embarrassed.

Speech Problems

There are teenagers out there that have speech impediments such as stuttering. Speech impediments can be difficult to deal with for many reasons and thus contribute to someone's social anxiety. Having a speech impediment may also decrease someone's confidence and thus make them want to avoid speaking to others. If you have a speech problem, know that your speech impediment does not make you any less of a person or invalidate your talking points. Your speech impediment is something that needs to be embraced and accepted by society and is not something you should be ashamed of at all. You deserve to feel confident when speaking regardless of your speech problems, and you will learn how to increase your confidence in a later chapter.

Genetics

There are also other causes that lead to social anxiety, such as inherited causes or genetics. If you have a family history of anxiety, you may be more likely to experience social anxiety and other anxiety disorders. Although there is no single specific number that indicates this genetic risk, experts approximate that the heritability of anxiety ranges from 30% to 50%, and many genes are linked with anxiety and other stress-related illnesses (Lindholm et al., 2020).

Unique Brain Structure

Another possible cause of social anxiety involves having a unique brain structure. The amygdala controls the human fear response, and so research indicates that a hyperactive amygdala can make you more vulnerable to anxiety. In addition, neurodiverse individuals (people with ADHD, autism, OCD, or any other condition that leads to people's brains having variations) are also known to have higher levels of social anxiety and overall anxiety. Specifically, autistic teenagers have a rather high likelihood of experiencing social anxiety. This is because autistic teens often struggle with social cues and with reading other people, and also become more quickly exhausted by social situations. According to the National Autistic Society, autistic teenagers may struggle to make friends, not look for comfort from others, seem insensitive, want to spend time alone if they become overloaded by others, and may behave in "socially inappropriate" manners. Autistic people may have a hard time socializing because they analyze past interactions and overthink social situations. However, they can overcome these challenges, feel confident socializing, and tackle their social skills, but this can take time and may happen in their late teenage years (Russell, 2022).

Social Anxiety is Treatable

Fortunately, social anxiety is treatable and has many different effective treatments. Mental health practitioners can create a solid plan for overcoming social anxiety, which is why I recommend you seek out mental health help if possible. Among the many effective treatments for social anxiety are psychotherapy, (which involves CBT and DBT, which I will talk more about in later chapters), and exposure-based therapy. You can also add to your therapies by implementing lifestyle changes. These changes can be implementing hobbies, exercising, maintaining a healthy diet, and researching herbal medicines and other homemade remedies. These changes can give you relief from your anxiety and can greatly help you since they can heavily affect your self-esteem, general welfare, and self-confidence (Paradigm Treatment, n.d.).

Medication for SAD

Antidepressant medicines can be given to teenagers that have been diagnosed with Social Anxiety Disorder, especially if the distress they feel is impairing and affects how they function. It is usually best to combine medication with therapy. SSRIs (selective serotonin reuptake inhibitors) are the types of psychiatric medications that are most commonly given to patients. SSRIs function by making serotonin re-absorption work slower. You can think of serotonin as a chemical postman (or neurotransmitter if you want to use the scientific term) that is responsible for the regulation of anxiety and mood. This is why serotonin is heavily associated with happiness (Russell, 2022). You can talk to your parents, primary care doctor, and therapist to see if taking antidepressants might be a good fit for you if you feel like your social anxiety is unmanageable even with psychotherapy.

Social Phobia vs. Shyness

It is totally normal for you to feel shy or self-conscious when you are around others. Shy people may feel awkward or uncomfortable if they are surrounded by strangers and may not want to engage in social situations. There is also anxiety that goes with being self-conscious or shy, and this anxiety can be extreme for some people. However, if you feel so anxious and self-conscious that it stops you from speaking up or socializing most of the time, it is likely that you have social anxiety and are not just shy. SAD is different from shyness since it is a recurring fear that impacts your school or work life, your confidence in yourself, your relationships, and your everyday activities. Social anxiety can go unnoticed if parents and teachers view a teenager as shy (Guy-Evans, 2022).

In addition, socially anxious people may see themselves as introverts even though they have SAD, and some parents with introverted children may fear that their child has social anxiety. Introversion and social anxiety are separate, which is why everyone needs to communicate to avoid misinterpreting SAD with introversion. Introversion is more of a spectrum and less of a characteristic since some teenagers show introversion and extraversion in distinct manners and levels that vary depending on their situation, and this is normal and healthy. However, social anxiety makes teenagers feel embarrassed or even paranoid, which is why this is an impairing mental health condition. Introverted people often prefer having more private lives with less friends, but people with SAD find it extremely difficult to become friends with other people (Paradigm Treatment, n.d.).

Signs and Symptoms

Accessing a social anxiety diagnosis is not always viable, especially if you live in a country like the United States that lacks universal healthcare and thus has high and unaffordable costs for psychiatric and psychological care and diagnosis. More and more people are turning to self-diagnosis because of monetary issues like this one, and self-diagnosis is a perfectly valid way of identifying if you have a certain mental disorder. This is why I have listed the criteria for SAD as it is found in the Diagnostic and Statistical Manual of Mental Disorders. The DSM-5 criteria involve:

- Having a solid fear or anxiety concerning one or more social situations that have the possibility of facing scrutiny from other people

- ○ Examples of this include social interactions such as meeting strangers or having a conversation, performing or presenting in front of an audience, and being watched (such as when drinking or eating)

- ○ In children and teenagers, this social anxiety has to take place among their peers and not just during interactions with grown-ups

- ○ This person is afraid that they will be negatively looked upon (such as being rejected or humiliated, or offending others)

- The social situation in question needs to almost always incite anxiety or fear

  - ○ In children and teenagers, this can be seen through freezing, crying, shrinking, having tantrums, clinging, or not speaking while socializing

- This fear is disproportionate to the person's sociocultural context and to the threat that the situation poses

- The social situations are either experienced with extreme anxiety or fear or avoided altogether

- This avoidance, anxiety, or fear causes distress that is clinically significant and that results in the deterioration of how that person functions socially, occupationally, or in any other area of functioning

- The avoidance, anxiety, or fear persists and lasts for at least six months or longer

- The avoidance, anxiety, or fear cannot be explained better by another mental health disorder such as Generalized Anxiety Disorder or depression

- The avoidance, fear, or anxiety is not related to any other medical condition that the person has or is excessive (Substance Abuse and Mental Health Services Administration, 2016)

Read over this list and see if these statements resonate with you. If more of those statements resonate with you than not, there is a good chance that you have Social Anxiety Disorder. Also, keep in mind that you can have social anxiety without necessarily having SAD. This may be true if you find that you resonate with many of these statements, but your distress is not enough to be considered clinically significant, or if you have had it for less than six months.

There are also other signs and symptoms that may indicate if you have social anxiety. You may have social anxiety if you:

- feel inhibited or self-conscious

- avoid socializing or social gatherings

- have a hard time making friends and maintaining your friendships

- have anxiety-related physical symptoms such as:

  - stomachaches

  - sweating

  - fast heartbeat

  - shaking

  - tense muscles

  - blushing

- struggle to start a conversation

- are afraid of being embarrassed

- self-sabotage yourself by thinking or behaving in ways that stop you from doing what you want to do

- pull out of clubs or extracurriculars

- criticize yourself or judge yourself negatively

- have panic attacks

- have anxiety or worry symptoms arise before a social event

- have a low intellectual, emotional, and physical opinion of yourself

- are uncomfortable with being in social settings

- have adverse feelings towards social gatherings

- act irrationally so you can get out of social situations

- feel anxious when introducing yourself or when talking to others in private

- dread future social gatherings

- talk little about yourself when you are interacting with someone else

- are afraid to ask other people to hang out

- feel anxious about being around others

- stutter, mumble, or speak in a soft manner

- fear contributing in class or speaking up during it

- don't ask your teachers for help even if you are having a hard time with the course material

- are visibly uncomfortable when performing in front of others

- avoid your classmates when you are not in school

- play or eat alone

Socially Anxious Safety Behaviors

Other signs of social anxiety can be seen through safety behaviors that teenagers like you use. Safety behaviors actually worsen the social anxiety cycle, which is why you need to watch out for them. The following are some examples of safety behaviors:

- Engaging in something else (such as being on your phone) instead of being a part of a conversation

- Trying to please others all the time

- Pulling your hair over your face

- If you are neurotypical (or not neurodiverse), avoiding eye contact

- Giving in to pressure from your peers

- Talking really softly

- Constantly looking for approval or reassurance

- Making up reasons that justify not being in social situations

- Repeatedly looking at how you look in the mirror (Russell, 2022)

Key Takeaways

- People with social anxiety disorder (SAD), or social

phobia, experience intense fear and worry about being judged, rejected, or embarrassed by others. This can cause significant distress and can interfere with daily life.

- While there is no single factor that solely causes SAD, different aspects like brain chemistry, environment, and genetics can play a part.

- There are many ways to treat social anxiety, and mental health practitioners can help make a plan that works for you.

- Social Anxiety Disorder, unlike shyness, is a recurring fear that limits your ability to succeed academically or professionally, harms your self-esteem, strains your relationships and makes completing routine tasks difficult.

- The Diagnostic and Statistical Manual of Mental Disorders can help you determine if you have SAD by providing criteria for diagnosis.

Chapter 2

What Social Skills Do You Need as a Teen?

What social skills do you use in your day-to-day life? Do you believe these are important? Perhaps, or perhaps not. What would your life be like if you had no social skills at all? Would it be the same? Chances are this would not be so. Without social skills, you would be unable to hold most of the interactions that you experience in your daily life. You may think that you have no social skills already, especially if your social anxiety restricts them and/or you happen to be a quiet and reserved introvert, but this is not true. You may have underdeveloped or lacking social skills, but you must still have some portion of social skills, no matter how small, or otherwise, you would not be able to interact with the world as you do now. Talking with your family during dinner would become a Herculean task of some sort without the social skills that you already have. Asking the cafeteria lady at your school for some meatloaf would be nearly impossible if you absolutely had zero social skills. Without social skills, your social relationships with others might as well be nonexistent. Participating in group projects would be unthinkable, and asking out your crush (if you have one) would definitely be out of the question. The fundamental truth is that your life would be drastically different from what you know if you had no social skills at all. Whether you realize it or not you probably already have a few social skills, it may just be that you do not know how to use them or that they are inexperienced.

There are always bound to be exceptions to this rule. For instance, there are some folks on the autistic spectrum that may be non-verbal, but even then, many non-verbal autistic people are still able to communicate and use whatever social skills they may have through sign language or through accessible technology that has text-to-speech functions. There are also autistic people that are semi-verbal, meaning that they are sometimes non-verbal, but they can speak during some times as well.

A remarkable exception to this rule involves the case of Genie, which is rather famous in the field of sociology. Genie (the name she was assigned to guard her identity) had suffered through one of the worst cases of child abuse in the United States. Her father put her into a straitjacket that he made himself and tied her to a chair in a room inside their house. Genie was not allowed to make noise, speak, or cry, and her father had beaten and brutalized her multiple times. Genie came into the custody of Los Angeles welfare officers as a 13-year-old, and the officers found that she was unable to speak. She could say a few words such as "go," "mother," and "blue," but stayed silent most of the time. Thus, she had no social skills when she became a ward of the state of California. With the help of many experts, she was able to learn how to dress up, chew, and play, and she also grew her vocabulary. But she remained unable to make full sentences and use grammar, which is why many scholars argue that people cannot acquire language after a specific age (Carroll, 2016). Thus, Genie is an exception to the rule that I introduced, which says that most people already have existing social skills, no matter how underdeveloped. She was unable to form these social skills because of the circumstances surrounding her traumatic and abusive childhood.

Unlike Genie, it is very likely that you already have social skills. However, your social anxiety may be repressing them, or perhaps you need to work on them more. This chapter will elaborate on social skills, what they are, and what their role is. I will also talk about how having underdeveloped or inexperienced social skills affects you. Keep on reading to find out more about these topics.

What Are Social Skills?

Social skills are methods for establishing and maintaining interaction with others, as well as behaviors that are required to do so. They are also needed to maintain older relationships. Social skills can involve things such as making friends, tackling bullying, and starting a conversation. Lacking social skills or having underdeveloped social skills is believed to indicate that someone is neurodiverse and/or autistic, but this is not always true.

This is because some people do not naturally understand social cues and behaviors if they are impulsive or if they are hooked on gossip. However, people that are depressed, anxious, autistic, or have ADHD or other neurodiverse conditions may struggle with social skills and with how they relate to other people since the symptoms within their conditions can become challenges for them within social interactions.

According to experts, the four types of social skills are:

- Survival skills, which involve following instructions and directions, ignoring, and carefully listening to other people through active listening

- Interpersonal skills like turn-taking, starting or joining a chat, and sharing information about yourself and your views

- Conflict-resolution skills include learning how to lose and how to be a good sport, coping with bullying and teasing, and dealing with pressure from your peers

- Problem-solving skills, such as choosing what you should do or what the right decision is, knowing when you should apologize, and asking others for help

Teenagers can teach themselves social skills by focusing on behaviors that they desire and focusing on how they want to act instead of focusing on how they don't want to act. For example, you can research phrases that you can use to start a conversation instead of telling yourself something like, "I should stop ignoring people when they talk to me." You also need to allow yourself time to practice since social skills can take time to learn and they are increasingly complex. Teenagers can show improvements in their social skills if they are under the right conditions, but it is very hard for someone to get better at social skills if they cannot practice. You should look for professional help if you still find social skills hard after your parents and teachers try to help you, struggle with pressure from your peers, are shy or impulsive around other people, have conflicts with other teenagers or struggle with bullying, or have a hard time making social choices (Lake, 2018).

You use social skills when you interact and communicate with other individuals, and this communication can be verbal or non-verbal. Non-verbal communication includes aspects of communication such as body language, gestures, eye contact, and how you look. You do this because humans are extremely sociable beings that have come up with innovative and new ways to express their ideas and how they think and feel with others. For instance, in today's world, it is very likely that a teenager such as yourself is engaged in social media platforms such as Facebook, Twitter, Instagram, and TikTok. These social media platforms have therefore become a way in which modern humans express themselves by using their social skills.

What you say is impacted by your words and how you say them. The volume of your speech, your tone, the vocabulary you use, and also more subtle aspects such as gestures, body language, and other non-verbal ways of communicating all affect the delivery of your message. It is said that some people are better at socially interacting than others, and this has fascinated psychologists, scientists, and researchers who have explored how social skills function and what their nature is. To develop social skills, you need to be aware of the way in which you talk to other people. You can improve how you communicate and the ideas you deliver by ensuring effective and efficient communication.

Social skills also have several traits that define them. One of them is the fact that your social skills are directed by your goals. For instance, you may put more effort into your social skills and into behaving in a more friendly manner if you are around someone that you want to be friends with, or around someone that you need something from. People also can use more than one type of action for the exact same goal during the same time, which is why another trait of social skills is that they are related to each other. Social skills are actions that judge people into how skilled they are at social interactions. These skills can also be obtained through learning and practicing them, especially if it is from a teacher or from an experienced communicator. Another trait of social skills is that they should be controlled by the person that uses them. When you learn social skills, you also learn when you should use certain actions, how to use these actions, and which ones to use.

A trait of social skills I will elaborate more on is the fact that social skills depend on the context in which the communication takes place. There is a difference between communicating professionally and communicating personally, and you should use distinct social skills for each method (Skills You Need, n.d.). When using personal communication, you usually connect with others and find value in that connection. You do this because connecting in this way makes you feel in a pleasant way. When you communicate personally, you want what is best for the other person, are present for them, and care for that individual. You should be direct and open when you communicate personally since in these relationships the goal is to be liked as who you really are. By communicating personally, you get to know the other person and observe how they act. This will create trust in the long term. You want to be intimate with others when you use personal communication. However, this means that there are some risks that you run into when you communicate personally. The risks are facing disappointment or hurt, and your pride is at stake in this type of communication.

On the other hand, professional communication differs from personal communication on some key points. When you communicate professionally you can be fond of the other person and still support them and look out for them, just like you would look out for someone that you communicate personally with. However, the motivations in professional communication are different because this communication aims to help you be successful at your job or school. You should communicate personally when you want things such as love and meaningful connections, and you should communicate professionally when you want to achieve a professional goal. You need to have a strategy when it comes to professional communication since the goal is for others to like you without being well-known. Unlike personal communication, which strives for intimacy, you need to avoid sharing too much when you communicate professionally since what you share may be used to hurt you. You should be skeptical and only trust people to a certain point when you use professional communication. This is because you do not know how much care the other person feels towards you. The risks you take in professional communication involve damaging your reputation or even losing your job if this is a relationship at your work. This is why you should remember that the people you communicate professionally with are not your intimate friends or family members (Sirota, 2014).

The Importance of Social Skills

Social skills are extremely important for teenagers to develop, and they have been shown to predict a person's future success. Research from Duke University and Pennsylvania State University indicates that having good social skills quadrupled young people's chances of graduating from college. Social skills also have positive associations with emotional well-being, independence, and success in the workplace. This is because having social skills leads to people having an increased ability to solve problems, observe, and react in social situations. Social skills can absolutely be learned through the efforts of teachers, mental health practitioners, and parents, whether they work collaboratively or independently to teach you social skills. There are distinct types of social skills, and you need to know which area you need help in (Lake, 2018).

Social skills are also incredibly important because of the many benefits and advantages that they can give you. Here are five different perks that result from having good social skills:

Improved Relationships

People with better social skills have more charisma, and this is a characteristic that is desired by many. Other people have a higher interest in charismatic folks since they show more interest in other people. This is very important because if you do not have strong relationships with others, you cannot go far in your life. When you focus on your relationships you are more likely to have better grades, find a job, and have friends. Also, the more improved relationships you have because of social skills will lead to you having higher self-esteem and can help decrease your stress.

Improved Communication

Having social skills also improves your communication skills. If you relate with others and are able to work in big groups, this will make you a better communicator. This is because it is impossible for someone to have excellent social skills without also having excellent communication skills. These communication skills can help you voice how you think, and they may be one of the most crucial skills you can have.

Higher Efficiency

Good social skills help you avoid those that you are not as fond of. You may not look forward to social interactions if they involve being around people that have viewpoints and interests that conflict with yours. After all, it can be easier to go to class if you know some of your classmates. Having good social skills can help you kindly tell that person you don't like at lunch that you want to be with other students.

Better Career Opportunities

Even though you are a teenager that is in school, having better career opportunities will always be a good thing in the long run for you. A lot of jobs require social skills since they may have you interact with your coworkers and clients. It is very unlikely that you will be able to succeed at your job if you are isolated. Many workplaces actively seek people with good social skills that can get along with others and motivate them.

More Happiness

Having good social skills can boost your satisfaction and happiness levels and make you have a more positive attitude towards your life. This is because successfully relating to others can open a lot of opportunities for you. For instance, if you are confident enough to start talking in a class discussion, this can lead to you getting a higher grade in that class. Saying hi and smiling at another person can end up in you becoming friends with them (Skills You Need, n.d.).

Your parents may want to enroll you in a social skills group because social skills are such a crucial element in people's lives. These groups are an amazing opportunity for you to learn social skills since they include role-playing, team activities, modeling, straightforward instructions, and positive reinforcement. There are many different kinds of social skills groups, and it is important that you and your parents find the right one for you. This group should be designed for teenagers around your age, and it should also focus on your specific social skills concerns. You and your parents can always consult with the social skills group facilitator to go over anything you have questions about before you join a group, and you can also consult this with your therapist if you have one (Lake, 2018).

Effect of Inexperienced Skills

You don't have to be a social butterfly because everyone has their own personality that shapes how they relate to other people. However, having positive relationships in your life will help you thrive and grow as a person. If you have social skills that have been well-developed you have a higher chance of gaining confidence from your ability to fulfill tasks and approach situations in a more successful manner. As a teenager, it is important that you notice and analyze any struggles you may have. Bullying, social isolation, rejection from your peers, conflicts, anxiety, anger, and poor grades can all point out the fact that you may have underdeveloped social skills. Noticing these issues can help if you let your teachers, parents, and other professionals know so that together you can all make a plan to improve your social skills and behavior. This will also help you feel better as well. If you leave any social skills and interaction struggles unattended these problems can remain there as you grow up and can significantly deteriorate your performance at school, your social interactions, and even your ability to prosper as an adult and get a job (Lake, 2018). They can also prevent you from making new friends and from keeping the older friends that you already have.

Role of Social Skills

Social skills have a powerful role in your life since they prepare you for your future life since they get you ready for healthier interactions during your lifetime. This is because having good social skills means that you will have better relationships with your peers as you grow older. When you learn social skills, they become a part of how you behave. This in turn helps you through your interactions with people that are in different sectors.

Social skills play a key role in your education since studies have indicated that social skills are extremely important in schools. Learning social skills effectively in your school improves your performance in school, especially during school projects in which you have to work with other students. Social skills allow you to get your message across in a polite manner, and they also help lessen the stress you may have from your exams, assignments, and quizzes. When you use your social skills when working with others and/or studying among a group, this can lead to more friendships. Good social skills can help you while you are presenting in front of your classmates and may also help you during class debates or school competitions. Having good social skills leads to having healthy relationships with your classmates, and this can help counteract any academic stress you have. This is because focusing on your relationships with your friends can make you feel more satisfied and give you a more positive perspective on your life.

Students usually cannot be isolated in their school and get good grades, which is why most schools (including colleges and universities) may look for students with social skills that are oriented by their goals. Thus, having good social skills can help you get into college and therefore have better career prospects. Social skills also reduce your levels of emotional pain and distress. People also become more ethical if they have better social skills, and they also acquire more respect in society because of that (Sharna, 2019). Therefore, the role that social skills play both in school and in the wider realm of society is extremely important.

Key Takeaways

- Social skills are integral to living a successful life, as they enable you to hold meaningful interactions with others.

- According to experts, there are four types of social skills namely survival skills, interpersonal skills, conflict-resolution skills, and problem-solving skills.

- Social skills are key for teenagers to develop, as they have been shown to predict a person's future success.

- You will have a greater chance of gaining confidence

from your capacity to complete tasks and approach circumstances in a more successful way if you have well-developed social skills.

- Social skills affect all aspects of your life, from preparing you for future interactions to helping you establish healthier relationships.

Chapter 3

The Most Effective Therapy for Your Social Anxiety

Cognitive Behavioral Therapy (CBT) is an evidence-based treatment that is known for being the gold standard of treatment for multiple mental illnesses. In other words, CBT is the chosen treatment for a variety of mental health illnesses, and this is because of how effective it is. Research indicates that CBT is by far the most effective way to treat depression and anxiety. Once someone has completed 5 to 15 modules of CBT, their CBT treatment has an effectiveness of 50—75% when it comes to defeating anxiety and depression. In addition, 82% of people that use CBT are likely to adhere to their plan of treatment (Pun, 2019). CBT surpasses the performance of other types of treatments for anxiety, and it also has the smallest rates of relapse in mental health treatment (Cognitive Behavioral Therapy Los Angeles, n.d.). A meta-analysis (or an analysis of multiple research studies) also indicated that CBT obtained higher rates of responsiveness than other comparison treatments in seven different studies. This is exactly why psychologists say that CBT has a firm and powerful evidence base (Hofmann et al., 2012).

After reading these statistics on the effectiveness of CBT it should be evident that it is a treatment that can benefit you. Social anxiety is a type of anxiety after all, and as you saw CBT has had great success in treating anxiety. This is why I will explain what CBT is in this chapter so that you can be familiarized with it and hopefully be encouraged to seek a therapist that specializes in CBT. However, do not worry if you are unable to afford therapy or otherwise cannot visit a therapist. This chapter will also teach you CBT techniques that you can do yourself to help with your social anxiety.

What is CBT?

You must first understand what CBT is before I go into the details of what CBT treatment for social anxiety entails. CBT stands for Cognitive Behavioral Therapy, and it is a form of treatment that is used to treat a wide variety of mental health issues such as anxiety disorders, substance use problems, depression, eating disorders, marital conflicts, as well as mental illnesses that are more severe like schizophrenia. There has been a lot of progress in CBT through clinical practice and research, and as I already mentioned it has a strong evidence basis.

CBT has several main concepts surrounding it. The first concept states that mental health issues are partially grounded on maladaptive or unhelpful thinking patterns. An example of an unhelpful thinking pattern involves telling yourself something such as, "I can't tell my group project partners my idea because I will just embarrass myself and my partners will laugh at me." A second CBT concept is that mental health issues are also partly grounded on patterns of behavior that do not help the individual, and these behaviors can be brought on by unhelpful thinking patterns. In the previous scenario you would not share your idea with your group and your partners may notice that you do not participate. The third concept in CBT is that your thinking and behavior patterns will continue if you do not control them and will carry over to other aspects of your life. For instance, you could stop sharing your ideas in different scenarios and may doubt that you have anything to contribute, so you would avoid others because you fear being rejected or embarrassed. A fourth CBT concept entails that mentally ill people can find healthier coping mechanisms for their mental health issues by increasing their life's effectiveness and finding relief for their symptoms (American Psychological Association, 2017). Mentally ill people can also cope by recognizing and changing their thoughts to become more helpful. Acknowledge that your ideas are valuable or that people will usually not laugh at you if you mess up while you speak (Raypole, 2021).

CBT is made up of two different components, the cognitive component and the behavioral one. The cognitive component of CBT uses strategies such as:

- Problem-solving through challenging circumstances

- Increasing the patient's self-confidence

- Better understanding why others behave as they do and understanding what motivates them

- Recognizing distorted thinking that is problematic and viewing these thoughts through a more realistic perspective

The behavioral component of CBT includes strategies such as:

- Calming and relaxing yourself

- Role-playing through interactions

- Not avoiding your fears and facing them instead

Keep in mind that CBT does not always use all of these strategies since the patient and therapist collaborate to create a treatment plan and understand the problem. CBT is a way of helping people become their own psychologists since people can learn to alter their troublesome feelings, behavior, and ways of thinking and understand coping mechanisms. CBT psychologists do not focus as much on what caused people's troubles and instead focus on what is currently happening in their patient's life. They do need some information about their patient's history, but most of their energy is devoted to progressing by developing healthier coping methods for life (American Psychological Association, 2017).

CBT assumes that people's thoughts influence their behavior and feelings, and that people's behavior influences what they feel and think. People's feelings influence their thoughts and behavior as well (National Social Anxiety Center n.d.). CBT bases itself on the premise that your feelings, thoughts, behaviors, situation in life, and biology are affecting each other. This is why CBT therapists believe that changing your thoughts and behavior can help improve how you feel and help you accomplish your goals if you struggle in a specific area.

CBT therapists help their patients identify the harmful cycles they are in, such as cycles that consist of distorted thinking, damaging beliefs, hurtful emotions, and self-defeating acts. These cycles can contribute to your personal issues and can leave you stuck in them. A CBT therapist will help you break free of those cycles by showing you how to use CBT strategies and skills that you will learn through practice. These strategies and skills are very specific and they will help you fulfill your goals and get rid of your personal issues. However, CBT does take a lot of devotion and hard work from both you and your therapist. By committing yourself to CBT by doing your therapy homework you can make lots of progress in a couple of months. This is because CBT is the most effective way to treat social anxiety. Another great thing about CBT is that you can keep using the strategies and skills you gain to fulfill other goals and deal with future troubles once you are done with therapy (National Social Anxiety Center, n.d.)

Internet CBT for Social Anxiety

CBT can also take place on the internet, also known as i-CBT. Online CBT is quickly gaining popularity and research seems to support it as well. i-CBT can even be more efficacious when you combine it with the support of a therapist or mental health practitioner. CBT has a very structured format, which means that it can be used online and as a self-help mechanism as well as a therapeutic intervention. Online CBT can help people whose extreme social anxiety stops them from leaving the safety of their homes and going to in-person therapy (Cuncic, 2021).

Goals of CBT for Social Anxiety Disorder (Does it Fit Your Condition?)

CBT aims to help patients identify when their beliefs and thought patterns are irrational so that they can replace these with more realistic thought patterns and behaviors. Your emotions, thoughts, and behaviors are all connected to each other, which means that people with social anxiety can change the way they act and feel by identifying thoughts that are not helping them. CBT for SAD works on a variety of different problematic areas, such as:

- Negative beliefs people with social anxiety face about their worth as a person and their abilities

- Teaching SAD patients how to become more assertive

- Anger, feelings of embarrassment, shame, or guilt that people with social anxiety feel because of past situations

- Addressing perfectionistic tendencies and replacing them with more realistic ones

- Erroneous beliefs that make SAD patients think that others are judging or criticizing them

- Working with procrastination that stems from SAD

If you are able to acquire a therapist that applies CBT for social anxiety, you may find that your CBT sessions can mimic a teacher-student dynamic. Your therapist takes on the role of a teacher by informing you of the basic CBT concepts and aiding you through your self-discovery and change road. CBT therapy sessions often assign homework, and working on these homework assignments is critical for the patient's progress (Cuncic, 2021).

Cognitive Techniques

CBT has a large focus on changing a patient's troublesome thinking patterns since these lead to the patient's anxiety. Cognitive techniques can help decrease your anxiety and increase your control of social interactions. People that struggle with social anxiety often have to deal with automatic negative thoughts that are not based on reality. These thoughts are a big hurdle in SAD precisely because they decrease your coping abilities and increase your social anxiety. For instance, people that have social anxiety around public speaking may find that they feel afraid of failing or face thoughts of being embarrassed just by thinking about being in a public speaking situation. CBT for SAD thus aims to substitute cognitive distortions like these with views that are more grounded in reality.

People that struggle with social anxiety may often be told that they need to "think positively," but their condition is much more complex than this. The problems underlying SAD are not so easily solved since if they were people with SAD would have conquered their social anxiety a long time ago. The human brain has a trait known as neuroplasticity, which means that the brain can change, alter, and adapt its function and structure as a response to the experiences it encounters throughout its life (Voss et al., 2017). This means that brains that suffer from social anxiety are hardwired to think in negative ways. This is why telling yourself statements such as "I won't be as anxious next time" will be ineffective because of the current way your brain thinks and operates. The good news is that because the brain has neuroplasticity and can therefore change the way it is arranged, people with SAD can gradually train themselves to think in a different way that is less negative. This is no easy task since changing negative automatic thoughts is something that takes repetition and practice on your part until your brain is habituated to your new way of thinking to the point in which it becomes automatic. As time goes by, the neural pathways and memory processes will shift in the brain of a person with SAD, which will lead them to feel, behave, and think in a different way (Cuncic, 2021).

Cognitive Restructuring

One cognitive technique you can use is identifying your problematic thoughts by using cognitive restructuring. Problematic thoughts are things such as hurtful self-talk, ideas, and mental images that make your anxiety worse. Cognitive restructuring is all about identifying distortions in your cognitions and thought patterns while you are in a social situation.

These distortions can include:

- overgeneralizing

- thinking in all or nothing

- overlooking the positive aspects of things, also known as mental filtering

- seeing your feelings as truths, also known as emotional reasoning

- catastrophizing

One way you can perform cognitive restructuring is by learning to compare your problematic thoughts to your real life (National Social Anxiety Center, n.d.). Ask yourself if there is any real-life evidence behind your socially anxious thoughts. For example, do you have any evidence that you will embarrass yourself in a certain social scenario, such as a private conversation? The answer to this question will most likely be a "no" since every conversation is different and most importantly, it has not happened yet so there is no way for you to know the outcome.

Another method of cognitive restructuring involves building a more helpful, compassionate, and realistic attitude about the social scenarios that you are in. For instance, instead of telling yourself things such as "I'll fail miserably at this public speaking event," you can hold a compassionate attitude towards yourself by telling yourself a statement such as, "Although I know this is very hard for me, I'm going to do the best I can in this presentation and that will be enough. I don't need to be a perfect public speaker and it is okay if I mess up in some parts."

However, it should be noted that cognitive restructuring by itself cannot always entirely get rid of your problematic thoughts. Cognitive restructuring is often the first step in preparing people with SAD for experiments in which they test their newly found compassionate, realistic, and helpful attitude towards themselves and their situation versus their problematic thoughts. Socially anxious teenagers like you can do cognitive restructuring after a social situation that scares you or triggers negative emotions so that you can learn from this scenario and defeat your distress (National Social Anxiety Center, n.d.). Thus, by learning to change the way you think you can become less socially anxious.

Psychoeducation is another cognitive component since learning about social anxiety can make you see that your socially anxious distortions only prevent you from enjoying life and worsen your social anxiety. You already learned a great deal about social anxiety in chapter 1 so you have this part covered. To summarize, the main goal of cognitive techniques in CBT is to get a patient to alter their core beliefs that shape how they view their surroundings. This change in their interior core beliefs will result in their anxiety symptoms improving in the long term (Cuncic, 2021).

Behavioral Techniques

One main behavioral technique in CBT is systematic desensitization. Systematic desensitization is an aspect of CBT that concentrates on changing behaviors that stem from social anxiety. This involves training that is based on exposure that teaches you how to relax as you gradually face (or are exposed to) situations that provoke your social anxiety. Systematic desensitization helps people with SAD experience less fear of the situations that scare them over time.

Exposing someone with SAD to socially anxious situations have to be done in a very gradual way. People with social anxiety may be told that they need to encounter their face and "toughen up," but this is actually terrible advice because people with SAD already encounter their fears regularly. A therapist that is versed in CBT for social anxiety will gradually expose you to social situations you fear until they no longer make you afraid (Cuncic, 2021).

There are three steps in systematic desensitization: learning relaxation techniques, listing your fears, and exposure. The first step in systematic desensitization involves learning relaxation techniques. One relaxation technique you can use is deep breathing. This technique is helpful since people breathe shallowly and rapidly when they are anxious, which leads to a stress response that in turn only worsens people's anxiety. There are three steps in deep breathing:

- Taking deep and slow breaths with your nose

- Holding your breath for a couple of seconds

- Exhaling with your mouth

Another relaxation technique you can use is visualization. When doing visualization, you will want to imagine a scene that relaxes you and think of the sensations in that scene, such as smells and sights. For example, you can imagine yourself watching a sunset or visualizing yourself at the beach. There are many guided visualization meditations out there that can help you relax during systematic desensitization.

Progressive muscle relaxation is another relaxation technique you can learn. In this technique, you will tense your muscles and later relax them. Doing this can decrease any tension you may have in your muscles, and it can help you understand how your body feels when it is relaxed as opposed to when it is tense. By understanding this you will know when you begin to tense up as a reaction to fear or anxiety (Raypole, 2019). This technique is very helpful since people with anxiety disorders may often have tense muscles.

This muscle tension may even feel normal to you if it is very automatic, which means that you may not remember what it is like to have your muscles relaxed (Ankrom, 2020). You can fix this by practicing progressive muscle relaxation. You can do this exercise on your own or with the help of a guided progressive muscle relaxation meditation that tells you which muscles you need to tense and relax.

The second step in systematic desensitization involves listing your fears. When doing this you should also be ranking them by their intensity. The third step involves facing exposure to what you fear. However, this part has to be done step by step, since harm can occur if it is not done this way. This gradual exposure through systematic desensitization can help you face social situations that you are scared of. If this exposure is not done step by step it can worsen your anxiety, increase your depression and self-doubt, and make you get stuck inside a vicious cycle (Cuncic, 2021). I will talk more about gradual exposure and how to engage in it in Chapter 6.

Another behavioral technique is making behavioral experiments (National Social Anxiety Center, n.d.). You can perform these as long as you feel like you are ready to do so. Remember, exposure has to be gradual, so make sure to prepare before engaging in any behavioral experiments! An example of a behavioral experiment would be going to a party and starting a conversation with some folks.

Keys to Success

There are several factors that can contribute to the success of CBT when treating social anxiety disorder. CBT is more likely to help patients that are willing to work on their homework assignments and that are able to face difficult and uncomfortable thinking patterns. This likelihood also depends on what the patient expects about their success in the treatment. Hard-working patients that believe that CBT can assist them to have a higher chance of recovery and improvement. CBT can be a rather intensive therapy that also demands the patient to actively participate, but as I already discussed at the beginning of the chapter, it ultimately is highly effective and shows long-lasting improvements. This is why all of this effort is worthwhile. Another key to success is to not force yourself into situations that scare you or make you socially anxious without preparing yourself since this can actually worsen your SAD. Overall, exposure therapy has a high level of efficacy in changing socially anxious acts and behaviors, but it is something that needs to happen one step at a time (Cuncic, 2021).

Key Takeaways

- Cognitive Behavioral Therapy, or CBT, is a form of treatment that is used to treat a wide variety of mental health issues including social anxiety.

- CBT focuses on assisting patients in recognizing when their ideas and thought processes are incorrect so that they may replace them with more accurate beliefs and actions.

- As a form of CBT, cognitive techniques can help

decrease your anxiety and increase your control of social interactions.

- A cognitive technique you can use to manage your thoughts is called cognitive restructuring. This involves identifying any distortions in your thinking pattern while you are experiencing a social situation.

- The process of systematic desensitization is one of the most important behavioral procedures in CBT, which focuses on changing social anxiety-related behaviors.

- Hard-working patients who believe in CBT have a higher chance of recovery and improvement.

Chapter 4

Tried-And-Tested Approach to Help Ease Your Social Anxiety

Dialectical Behavioral Therapy (DBT) is a psychological treatment that is strongly suggested for people with a variety of mental health problems. Many studies have concluded that training anxious individuals with DBT skills leads to better outcomes when compared to other treatments. DBT treatments that trained their patients with DBT skills were also found to have more effectiveness than DBT treatments that did not train their patients with DBT skills. This finding is the most relevant to you since social anxiety is a type of anxiety, and the research literature I just mentioned indicates that DBT is an effective treatment for anxiety.

However, DBT has also been found to be extremely effective for a variety of other conditions such as ADHD, disordered eating, Borderline Personality Disorder, and mood disorders such as depression and Bipolar Disorder. For instance, DBT has led to substantial improvements among individuals whose depression resisted treatment. These individuals fared significantly better when they were compared to other participants that were placed on a waiting list. DBT has proved itself to be effective when it comes to decreasing depression by the time the treatment is over. It also has been shown that it can greatly reduce mania as well (Harned & Botanov, 2016). In addition, DBT has proven to be extremely effective when it comes to treating the disorder it was intended to treat, which is Borderline Personality Disorder (BPD). Seventy-seven percent of DBT patients no longer have BPD after they have been treated with DBT for one year (Anwar, 2022).

What Is DBT?

DBT stands for Dialectical Behavior Therapy, and it is a different type of CBT. DBT is a type of talk therapy (or psychotherapy.) DBT's core goals are to help people create healthy coping mechanisms for stress, help with emotional regulation, show others how to live in the present moment and better their interpersonal relationships with other people.

Although DBT was designed to help patients with Borderline Personality Disorder (BPD), you do not need to have BPD to use DBT. As I already said in the introduction, DBT can be used to treat a variety of different mental health issues, including social anxiety. DBT helps those that struggle to regulate their feelings or have self-destructive tendencies (such as people that have substance use or eating disorders, as well as people that struggle with suicide attempts, self-harm, and suicidal ideation). DBT has also been employed as a treatment for Post-Traumatic Stress Disorder, or PTSD. Like CBT, DBT is an evidence-based therapy that can help a wide variety of mentally ill individuals.

DBT can be used in a variety of different settings, including:

- One-on-one therapy with a mental health practitioner in which DBT skills are tailored to the patient's personal life struggles

- Coaching over the phone allows patients to call their therapist outside of their therapy sessions to ask for coping advice if they are placed in a hard situation

- Group therapy—which is a space in which multiple patients are taught DBT skills within a group dynamic

- Online DBT courses that can be accessed through websites or mobile apps

What You Can Expect from DBT Therapy

You can expect for you and your therapist to achieve positive outcomes with DBT. Your therapist may do this by validating your feelings and actions. They may validate your behavior by acknowledging that your actions are understandable because of the context that you were in, but they will not always state that your actions were the best way to deal with that situation. This therapeutic approach can help lower your distress when you think about changes in your life and also improve your cooperation. In DBT you will learn a great deal about accepting your feelings, your life situation, how you feel, and overall accepting who you are. The DBT skills you learn will also result in positively changing how you interact with others and behave. DBT therapy will also allow you to identify destructive ways in which you act and help you substitute them in a healthier and more effective manner. You will also learn how to alter what you think and believe if those thoughts and behaviors are ineffective or do not help you. The DBT skills you will develop will also greatly improve what you are able to do. Lastly, DBT will also allow you to acknowledge the good things about yourself and encourage you to use these positive characteristics (Schimelpfening, 2022).

Main Concepts and Components in DBT

DBT has a few essential concepts that you need to know. One of them is that you are doing your best, and another one is that you need new manners to do your best and try more arduously. One last essential concept in DBT is that there are connections in every single aspect of your life. You cannot avoid change and this is the only constant thing in which you can find stability and thus trust. In addition, there are four main components in DBT. These components are individual therapy, therapy training as a priority, availability of help, and group therapy.

Individual Therapy

DBT sessions are usually weekly and involve a trained mental health practitioner. You will talk about your most critical issues with your DBT therapist if you have one. In DBT individual therapy you will investigate how what you believe, your expectations of your life, and your thinking patterns may make your difficulties more challenging. In this therapy, you can expect to find new methods of dealing with stressful situations (specifically social situations). You will also learn how to implement DBT skills that will make your world and reality a place you can properly function in. You will remain in therapy throughout the whole DBT process.

Therapy Training as a Priority

Psychology highlights the training DBT therapists have to take in order to be qualified to provide DBT services. DBT therapists must stay updated with newer research, findings, studies, and psychological treatment on DBT. There are many therapists that are trained in DBT since it is a type of CBT. If you want to expand your DBT skills beyond this book you may want to find a therapist that specializes in DBT. You can start doing this by telling your parents you want to see a DBT therapist so they can talk to your primary care doctor. Then your primary care doctor can refer you to a DBT therapist, or if you already have a therapist that doesn't specialize in DBT you can ask them to refer you as well. There are also online therapy spaces such as Talkspace and BetterHelp that offer DBT licensed therapists' services in a way that is affordable, easy, and from the comfort of your own home.

Availability of Help

If you use DBT in a traditional manner, then you will be able to contact your DBT coach via phone in between your therapy sessions. This coach can be a mental health practitioner such as a DBT specialized therapist, but they do not always have to be one. You are encouraged to contact your coach over the phone, but you should not abuse this, and your calls shouldn't be a habit. You can't constantly call your coach about things you are dealing with in therapy without trying to use DBT yourself. If your coach is your therapist, they may address if they feel like you are using these calls as a crutch.

Group Therapy

A lot of the time DBT will involve both individual and group therapies. DBT group therapies include discussions, chances to practice the DBT skills that you have learned, and lectures. Group therapy may happen weekly for five months. If you do have the opportunity to attend group therapy, it is imperative that you go to each therapy so that you can make the most out of it (Anwar, 2022).

Mindfulness

One technique that is used in DBT is mindfulness. DBT helps you develop mindfulness skills that help you live in the present moment. You probably already know that socially anxious people like you feel like their behavior is held to a high standard and that they are unable to meet these standards, which is why you may focus a lot on your own social performance and behavior.

This in turn increases your anxiety and may even be manifested visibly through physical symptoms like blushing and shaking that I previously listed, and this in turn may cause you to worry even more about how others are viewing you. Mindfulness is a way to break this self-focused attention cycle since it is all about describing and noticing what is happening to you. In mindfulness you can use your five senses to hear, see, smell, and feel the environment you are in so that your attention will not be fixated on your social performance. Mindfulness is a practice that needs you to be consistent, but it is very effective in breaking the social anxiety cycle (Hires, 2019).

Mindfulness is anchoring your attention to what is happening in the present moment. This technique helps you avoid living in the future or the past, and it is a huge pillar of DBT. In other words, mindfulness is all about setting aside your socially anxious thoughts by engaging with what you are currently doing, whether that is an activity of some sort or a conversation. This helps you get outside of your mind and get inside the moment you are living in, and this allows you to be more natural and comfortable in your interactions with others (National Social Anxiety Center, n.d.).

Mindfulness helps you realize what is going on inside of you in terms of sensations, feelings, emotions, and thoughts in a way that is curious and free of judgment. It also lets you identify what surrounds you in a non-judgmental way as well. When you are being mindful you should describe what is going on in a simple and easy manner that everyone (including you) can comprehend. Mindfulness teaches you how to be a part of behaviors that are goal-directed and based on your values (Anwar, 2022). Practicing mindfulness is a way to slow yourself down and better concentrate on healthy coping mechanisms whenever you are feeling distressed. Mindfulness can also prevent you from falling back on your impulses and going through automatic negative thinking.

You can practice mindfulness by paying attention to your breath and watching how your belly rises and falls with each breath. When doing this, ask yourself what the sensations of breathing feel like. Where in your body do you feel your breath the most strongly? Is your breath deep or shallow? Is it quick or slow?

There is no one way to practice mindfulness and there is certainly no wrong way to practice it. All being mindful means is that you are aware of your experience in the present moment and realize what arises during it. You can practice through guided mindfulness meditations and podcasts that are available online, and you can also practice being mindful during everyday activities such as washing the dishes or making your bed. Practicing mindfulness during these activities would mean being as fully present as you can be while you are performing the task. If you do notice that your mind tends to wander from the activity you are doing, you can simply remind yourself to come back to the present moment. You should do this in a gentle and caring way without becoming frustrated with yourself. Think of your attention as a puppy that wanders and forgets to bring back the ball you threw at it. You wouldn't scold the puppy for wandering, so you would not scold yourself either for thinking of something else during the activity.

Interpersonal Effectiveness

Interpersonal effectiveness is a DBT technique that goes after mindfulness, and it deals with how you can positively communicate with the people around you. This section of DBT teaches you how to cope with any struggles you encounter and how to manage your relationships. DBT teaches you to:

- communicate clearly

- get rid of hostility

- know how you can ask for your needs to be fulfilled without losing self-respect

- say no to others

You can use the acronym GIVE to positively change the way you communicate and to better your relationships:

- G—Gentle: Do not judge or attack other people and do not make threats

- I—Interest: Show that you are interested in what the other person has to say by truly being present and listening without interrupting other people so you can speak

- V—Validate: Recognize how the person you are talking to feels and thinks

- E—Easy: Aim to maintain an easy-going attitude by being light-hearted and smiling often if you can (Schimelpfening, 2022)

Distress Tolerance

Learning to tolerate distress involves accepting the changes in your life, and this concept is also known as radical acceptance. Radical acceptance is a key to overcoming emotional pain and it is one of the most important concepts in DBT. Practicing radical acceptance involves accepting the reality that you live in, investigating the underlying core beneath your emotional pain, appreciating and accepting your past and your current life even if things are not the way you want them to be, and being ready for occasional misfortune and being alright with that. Radical acceptance is all about not avoiding your pain and instead accepting that it is happening (Intrepid Mental Wellness, PLLC, n.d.). This concept teaches you that pain is not permanent and that you are going to be alright once it goes away (Anwar, 2022).

Another technique that can help you tolerate stress is learning to soothe yourself. Self-soothing techniques are able to calm down your emotions by grounding yourself through physical stimuli. You can do this through any of the five senses: smell, hearing, touch, sight, and taste. There are many ways to self-soothe and they all depend on what is most effective for you. Here are some different self-soothing ideas you can experiment with:

- being kind towards yourself

- imagining the face or voice of a loved one

- picturing your favorite place

- spending time with your pets (if you have any)

- planning fun activities

- making a list of your favorite things in different categories

- touching a comforting item (such as a stuffed animal)

- listening to music

- sucking on a piece of candy and noticing how it tastes and feels

- listing positive things about your life (Healthy@UH, 2020)

You can also try to distract yourself as a way to tolerate stress. Another helpful exercise you can do is using any kind of physical movement to put your body in charge. You can run the stairs up and down, go outside, or stand up from your seat and stroll around. The main idea here is that you can distract yourself by letting your body follow how you are feeling. You can also make a list of the pros and cons of a social situation that triggers your social anxiety. These distress tolerance strategies can help get you ready for difficult feelings and help you cope with them while having a positive long-term attitude (Schimelpfening, 2022).

Emotional Regulation

Emotional regulation is usually the last skill that is taught in DBT, but it is one of the most vital DBT skills in the training process. It can be really hard to control and regulate your emotions if you are an intense person, and this is especially true of teenagers like you since adolescence is a time filled with many challenges such as bullying and peer pressure. However, you can absolutely manage your emotions even in the midst of adolescence. Emotional regulation can help you when you are experiencing social anxiety and are feeling depressed, frustrated, overwhelmed, or angry because of it. Learning to regulate your emotions can help you be able to control them before they control you. Emotional regulation also increases your confidence in your capacity to manage your emotions and it also allows you to experience less vulnerability.

One exercise you can use to regulate your emotions is known as the opposite action exercise. The DBT skill of acting opposite to your emotions can be very effective since decreasing avoidant behaviors is extremely important to people that have social anxiety. In this exercise, you will identify your emotions and do the opposite of what they want you to do. For instance, if you are feeling depressed and that makes you want to isolate yourself from your loved ones, do the opposite and instead plan to see your friends and family (Schimelpfening, 2022).

You can also regulate how you are feeling by concentrating on your positive emotions instead. And there is also a process model that states how emotions come to be:

- Situation: Emotions can begin in an external situation (such as something someone said to you) or through your own thinking

- Attention: The situation makes you pay attention

- Appraisal: In this step, you appraise or assess what is happening

- Response: You can respond physically or emotionally

In emotion regulation, you can choose any given part of this model to change how you feel. In the situation stage, you can opt to participate in positive situations, change the way you act and therefore change the situation, or avoid people that you know are likely to hurt you. In the attention stage, you can redirect your attention to something else, such as someone's nonverbal cues or thinking about what they may actually be saying. In the appraisal stage, you can change how you think about what is happening by being aware that you are often making conclusions that may not happen. In the response stage, you can alter how you will respond to what is happening. For instance, you can do breathing exercises instead of screaming or lashing out, or you can take someone that cares for you with you instead of avoiding an unpleasant circumstance (Salters-Pedneault, 2022).

Keys to Success

The keys to success for DBT are relatively similar to the keys to success that I talked about for CBT. Like in CBT, some keys to success in DBT are your ability to face difficult and uncomfortable thoughts and hard work. Another key to success in DBT is to show up to your DBT therapy sessions if you have them. You should also make sure that you are really engaging in the mindfulness opening at the beginning of the therapy since these take place in a DBT group during the first five minutes. Another key to success is paying attention to the content that you learn in DBT since one can become easily distracted by their own thoughts. Also, make sure that you are taking notes since they can help you later. If you are in a DBT class you should also volunteer when the instructor gives people a chance to talk about any particular struggles (Debbie, 2012).

Key Takeaways

- Dialectical Behavior Therapy (DBT) is a different type of CBT that helps people develop healthy coping mechanisms for stress, emotional regulation, living in the present moment and improving interpersonal relationships.

- The skills you acquire through DBT will help you interact with others and act more positively, as well as allowing you to recognize harmful behaviors and assist you in replacing them in a healthier and more successful way.

- DBT helps you develop mindfulness skills that help you live in the present moment.

- Interpersonal effectiveness is a DBT technique that helps you to be mindful of how you communicate with the people around you.

- The ability to tolerate distress is an important aspect of overcoming emotional suffering, and it is one of DBT's most essential ideas.

- As a DBT skill, emotional regulation increases your confidence in your capacity to manage your emotions and it also allows you to experience less vulnerability.

- If you want to succeed in DBT, two essential keys are the willingness to face difficult thoughts and putting in some hard work.

Chapter 5

How to Build and Strengthen Your Social Skills

Building and strengthening your social skills is incredibly important for your well-being and success. Take a group school project for example. In a group school project, you will need to be able to interact with your group partners in order to get a good grade on your assignment. What will happen then if your social skills are not as good as they should be?

Having underdeveloped social skills could be detrimental for you from the very beginning. Sometimes teachers will allow students to pick their own group partners, and students with better social skills are more likely to get chosen to be in a group. Having weak social skills could mean that you are less likely to be chosen for a group, and therefore you could end up working with someone that you do not want to work with. Or even worse, you could end up with the person in the class that no one wants to work with because they are lazy and never pull their weight in group projects. This would be especially true if you have social anxiety and cannot bring yourself to ask others to work with you.

Once you start working on the actual project you may realize that your weak social skills may get in the way of the project. You may specifically notice that you lack the social skill of active listening. If you are not actively listening to your project partners, you may miss important details that they convey. For instance, by not actively listening you could miss your partner telling you that you need to work on a certain part of the project before a certain day to meet a deadline. Not listening to this part could have repercussions for your grade and it could also damage the relationship between you and your project partner.

Following directions and instructions falls under survival social skills as well. If there is a leader in your school group, you may find that they assign instructions to everyone so that the work is split evenly. Weak social skills may mean that you are unable to follow instructions very well. Therefore, not having strong social skills can also negatively impact your performance in a school group project.

Similarly, there are many ways in which problems can arise when working on a school project. You may have a disagreement with your partner on what your presentation should be about, or perhaps on how work is split out among the group. Problem-solving skills are essential social skills that could help you find solutions to problems like this. Conflict-resolution skills are also social skills that could help you when there is a disagreement within the group. Therefore, having weak social skills could also mean that you and your group are unable to sort out your differences, and this may negatively affect your school work and therefore your grades.

As you can see, having social skills can make or break your experience in a group project. It can also make or break your experience in many other aspects of your life. This is why I will be talking about how you can improve your social skills in this chapter.

Survival Social Skills

As I discussed in a previous chapter, listening is a survival social skill that you can enhance through active listening. Active listening specifically is an invaluable social skill since it makes other people feel like what they have to say is valued and heard. Active listening consists of a listening design that positively engages you with the person you are talking to. When you actively listen to someone you do more than just hear someone else talk. The following are active listening strategies that you can use in your daily communication with others.

Listen Attentively

Make sure you are paying attention when someone talks to you by giving them your undivided attention and listening with all of your five senses. This means you should not be on your phone and that you should avoid daydreaming. Also, make sure to cease your internal self-talk. You can also listen attentively by being mindful of nonverbal cues. Smile, try not to fold your arms, lean in, and nod at certain points. Try to avoid making negative facial expressions (such as frowning) and make eye contact while listening if it is appropriate in your cultural context. Neurodiverse folks may struggle with these last points, so if you are neurodiverse make sure to prioritize your well-being and do not force yourself to do these things if they cause you discomfort.

Reflect on What You Listened to

Instead of giving advice or your opinion, you can paraphrase what you have just been told. You can summarize what they told you and doing this helps the other person know that you understand and validate them.

Avoid Judgment

Try to keep a non-judgmental and neutral attitude when you talk to others, so they feel like they are able to open up. Your goal should be to make your conversation a safe zone that is free of blame, shame, or criticism.

Make Questions

You should ask questions that are open-ended to people when actively listening. Aim to not ask questions that can be answered with just a "yes or no."

Show Patience

You should listen with the intent to understand and not with the intent to respond. Avoid interrupting the other person, finishing what they are saying, filling moments of silence by talking, or topping the story with your experiences (Cuncic, 2022).

Another part of survival social skills is learning how to ignore someone if they

- talk badly about you.

- negatively interfere in your life.

- have views that clash with yours.

Although I ideally want to foster your social skills by having you interact with people, sometimes this is not possible. This is especially true if that person continues to hurt and mistreat you and/or is bigoted towards you if you are a member of a minority group. You can ignore someone without hurting them by:

- not doing eye contact with them

- not answering their calls and muting them on social media

- not behaving angrily towards them

- not using rude language and avoiding being rude overall

- not helping them if they ask you to

- if they call you by your name, pretending to not hear them

- persistently holding this attitude towards them so that they think this is how you normally behave (United We Care, 2021)

One last survival social skill involves being able to follow directions. These are some tips that can help you better follow directions:

- Ask specific questions about the directions you were given

- Know which is your learning style (auditory, reading, and writing, kinesthetic, or visual) and make sure your instructions match that style

- Practice by assigning directions to other people

- Avoid distractions

- Understand the context behind your directions

- See yourself following the directions and fulfilling their task

- Give yourself a pep talk (Gray-Grant, 2021)

Interpersonal Social Skills

One interpersonal social skill that you can use in your everyday life is knowing how to join a conversation. If you know what topics will be discussed in a certain conversation (for instance, if you're going to a book club meeting) then you should prepare by reading about those topics. You can also keep up with current events, follow popular topics, and read the news so you have topics to talk about in any given conversation.

The next step in joining a conversation is choosing which group of people you will talk with. You can join people that share similar interests as you or you can join a group in which there is an acquaintance or friend you already have. When you join a conversation, you should make sure to practice the active listening skills that I just talked about. Establishing eye contact is also a good idea if it is possible for you and socially acceptable in the cultural context that you are in.

You should also have a polite attitude when joining the conversation. You can do this by making a statement such as "Are you all talking about _____?" or "Can I ask a question?" Show that you are interested in the group and try hard to show that you care about what is being talked about. This is important since SAD may make you have a harder time during conversations. You can ask questions that invite everyone to share their experiences.

You can learn how to join conversations by using the acronym "CLASS":

- C—Choosing a group

- L—Listening

- A—Asking questions

- S—Showing interest

- S—Sharing about yourself (Cuncic, 2020)

Talking About Yourself

Sharing information with others is a great way to build an emotional link between you and another person, and it is an important interpersonal social skill. An acronym that can help you when you are deciding whether you should share information with someone is WAIT:

- W—Wanting to share information

- A—Appropriate circumstances

- I—Inoculating people

- T—Trust

Wanting to Share Information

Make sure that you actually wish to share information with other people, and know that you never have to share anything that is too personal or that makes you uncomfortable.

Appropriate Circumstances

It is important to keep in mind that there is an appropriate place and time for sharing information. For instance, if you have a part-time job you wouldn't share information about your sexual trauma with your boss (at least not unless you are reporting sexual harassment in the workplace).

Inoculating People

Ease others through what you share by giving them a small dose of information and seeing how they may react if you decide to share more information with them. This is known as "inoculating" others into information.

Trust

Also, make sure that the person you are sharing information with can be trusted. This is why some teenagers like you may save their personal experiences to share until their friendships and relationships are more developed (Carmichael, 2021).

Taking Turns in a Conversation

Learning how to take turns when talking to others is another crucial interpersonal social skill. Most talking turns have three parts:

- An opening that links this turn to the last one

- The content you are communicating

- The ending signals

You can tell when an ending signal is present if someone uses phrases such as "so" or "anyways...", or if they lower their voice when they finish their sentence. Your turns may be too long if people around you appear bored or annoyed, if people leave the conversation, or if others cut you off and you keep talking over them (Social Communication, n.d.).

How to Start a Conversation

Starting a conversation is another interpersonal social skill. You can start a conversation by inquiring people about information that they may know. For example, you can ask your classmate a question such as "Do you know when this homework is due?" Introducing yourself is always a good conversation starter, so you can say something like, "Hi, my name is _____, what is your name?"

Offering to help others when you can is another great way to build a conversation. You can also ask for help as a way to start a conversation. You may also bring up positive comments about a certain circumstance. You can also make an observation about a certain situation to start talking to someone. For instance, you can say something like, "I really liked the school dance yesterday!" Making small talk by talking about the weather is another way to start talking to someone (Indeed Editorial Team, 2019).

Verbal Communication

Verbal communication is another interpersonal social skill that you can develop. Here are some tips that can help you be an effective verbal communicator:

- Pause before speaking and think about what you are going to say

- Know who your audience is and keep that in mind

- Avoid interruptions

- Watch your tone and mimic other people's tones

- Talk confidently

Nonverbal communication is another interpersonal social skill. You can improve your nonverbal communication by having your body reinforce what you say. For example, you can nod and smile to let someone know that you understand them.

Here are some general tips that can help you improve your interpersonal social communication skills:

- Be conscious of your acts and think about yourself

- Try to establish a positive environment around you

- Show interest and concern for others

- Ask for constructive criticism on your interpersonal skills from your friends and family

- Do not try to push your opinions onto others (Kelly, 2021)

Problem-Solving Social Skills

One problem-solving skill involves asking for help when you need it. The first tip that you need to know when asking for help is that you need to be very specific when you ask for help regardless of whether you are asking for help in your classes, in extracurriculars, or in your personal life. The second tip you need to know is that you don't have to be ashamed or apologize for asking for help. Make sure that you ask for help in person and not over email or text, and try not to talk about how you can reciprocate. Lastly, you can follow up with the person you asked for help by letting them know how their help resulted (Davis, 2020).

Another part of problem-solving involves knowing when to apologize. You should apologize if you:

- yelled, teased, hurt, or disrespected another person

- did not do something you were meant to do

    - For instance, if you broke a promise or did not stick to your curfew

- lost or broke someone's belongings

- were harsh or unjust

- told a lie, spread hurtful gossip, purposefully broke a rule, or posted something that was hurtful (KidsHealth, 2022)

As a whole, there are five main steps that occur when doing problem-solving:

1. Assessing what caused the problem

In order to do this, you must obtain data, identify which situations may have led to the problem, and know what needs to be worked upon.

2. Coming up with interventions that can solve the problem

In this step you can brainstorm multiple solutions since having more than one intervention has you covered in case the first solution does not work out.

3. Assessing which intervention is the best one

When you assess which intervention is best you have to keep in mind factors such as any resources you may need and any possible costs and obstacles that stand in the way of your success.

4. Create a plan to implement this intervention

Once you know which solution you will use you can make the plan and establish benchmarks that will let you know if the plan is working or not.

5. Analyze how effective your solution was

Assess if and how the solution is functioning so that you know if you need to change the plan or if the problem has been dealt with. (Doyle, 2020)

Conflict Resolution Social Skills

Teenagers like you may often have to endure bullying and teasing as a part of their school experience, which is why it is critical that you develop your conflict resolution social skills. Conflict resolution skills can outline a plan that you can use for all of your life.

The Emphatic Process

One conflict resolution skill is known as the empathic process. This process is especially useful when you are arguing with family members, friends, or romantic partners. In the empathic process each person should spend a third of the time talking without defending themselves from the accusations that the other person says about them. Do not weaponize private information against the other person and try not to say hurtful things to them. If you hurt the other person's self-esteem you can win the battle, but you will lose the war. Give yourself a "time in" in which you can resort to the self-soothing coping mechanisms I covered in a previous chapter. Try to accept and respect the other person's differences without trying to change them. Recognize the differences between what you want and what you need so that you can have healthier interactions. Remain respectful and communicate in a way that is descriptive, clear, and calm. Aim to collaborate so everyone can find a solution to the issue (Gross, 2015).

Assertiveness

Another conflict resolution skill is known as assertiveness, and this is a skill that you can use against bullies (Lozano, 2019). Assertive teenagers know how to fend for themselves in a respectful way without being violent. Here are some ways to be more assertive:

- Using "I" statements instead of "you" statements

  - For instance, you can tell your bully something like, "I won't do your homework for you," instead of saying, "You are such a dumb and lazy student, that's why you bully me into doing your homework"

- Assessing your style of communication also helps you be more assertive

  - Do you speak your mind or stay quiet?

  - Are others intimidated or scared by you?

  - Do you quickly judge and blame others?

  - These are some questions you can ask yourself to assess your communication style.

- Rehearsing what you are going to say

- Starting by being assertive with people that are close to you at first

  - You can later use assertiveness against your bullies

- Controlling your emotions

- You can do this by using the emotional regulation DBT skills you previously learned

- Learning to say no

  - You do not have to explain why you say no and you can be direct (Mayo Clinic Staff, 2022)

Another common issue that you may face as a teen is peer pressure. Mastering your leadership skills is a great way to fight against peer pressure. By guiding your friends to do the right thing you can become a leader and a role model. Stay firm in your choices and do not be afraid to stand out from your group of friends. If you have firm values and beliefs that others cannot shatter, your friends and other people are likely to admire you. When you give into peer pressure you actually just become a follower instead of being "cool" (Lozano, 2019).

Another conflict resolution skill involves knowing how to lose and being a "good sport." You can do this by not arguing with authority figures such as sports coaches, and by following the rules of the competition. Knowing how to lose also means knowing how to win, since you should not be rubbing your victories onto everyone's faces. If you do lose, do not make excuses or whine. If you are in a competition, make sure you respect the opposing team and do not tease them. If applicable, helping a fallen player up is a way to be a good sport (KidsHealth 2019).

One last conflict resolution skill is known as nonviolent communication. In nonviolent communication, you communicate your needs and feelings to the other person and make a request of them in a way that is non-judgmental. You begin by making an observation that sticks to the facts and not to how you evaluate what happened. An example of this is saying something such as "I notice you borrowed my pen during class, and you didn't give it back."

Then you can express your feelings in a way that does not share your interpretation of these feelings. For example, you can say, "I feel annoyed when you don't give me my pen back." After that, you can express your needs, which should be a universal need that everyone has. For example, "I need to feel that my belongings are safe and I don't feel like my pen is safe if you don't give it back." Lastly, you can make a request that is not a demand. For instance, you can say, "Can you please give me my pen back?" (Kashtan & Kashtan, n.d.).

Key Takeaways

- Your social skills are integral to your success and wellbeing, so much so that having underdeveloped social skills could be detrimental.

- Being a good listener is an important social skill since it makes other people feel appreciated and heard.

- Knowing how to start a conversation is one social skill that you may apply in your daily life.

- Being able to ask for help when you need it and knowing how to apologize are two important problem-solving skills.

- It is critical that you learn how to resolve conflicts effectively so that you can create a strategy that works for all of your life.

Chapter 6

How to Overcome Social Anxiety

Tobias struggled with Social Anxiety Disorder for most of his life, and SAD impacted him so deeply that he had to take strong medication for it and receive disability benefits due to the social anxiety that he faced concerning job interviews. He spent 90% of his time feeling uneasy and had a very hard time being around people. Relaxing was definitely out of the question for him. However, he was able to heal from SAD, which is why I will be sharing his healing story to show you that overcoming social anxiety is possible.

Tobias was described as sensitive and shy when he was a child, and he himself believed that there was no way to fix this so he did not even try to do so. He gave up on himself from a very early age, telling himself that his genetic predisposition had doomed him to be shy. However, he had never even heard of SAD until he saw his first therapist, which is why he struggled for a long time. Tobias felt a lot of embarrassment and shame surrounding his SAD and he had been raised in a way that made him feel like he couldn't talk about his feelings without being weak. This is why he kept quiet and never looked for help or told anyone about his social anxiety for years. He felt like no one else could understand him, and when he did tell people many told him things such as "Man up," or, "You shouldn't care what other people think of you."

However, Tobias now understands that acknowledging your need for help and speaking up about how you feel is actually a rather brave thing to do. He believes that you need to ask for help in order to change. After all, no one will be able to assist you if you pretend that everything is okay. A lot of people with social anxiety suffer for 10 years before they look for psychological help. Social anxiety is treatable, which is why this does not make sense.

Tobias' life took a drastic change for the better when he asked for help. He saw a therapist and another person who had suffered from social anxiety. This person was able to convince him that he could defeat social anxiety. Everything began to change for him when he was finally able to believe that social anxiety is not a sentence for life.

His therapists helped him by telling him that he needed to stop self-deprecating by calling himself mean names such as "weird," "loser," and "ugly." With the help of his psychologists, he learned that no one can be perfect and that he does not have to be perfect.

He also learned that he could be accepted and liked even if he seemed awkward sometimes.

Tobias learned through his therapy sessions that he could find the validation and self-worth he needed in himself instead of seeking for other people's approval. He realized that he no longer cared as much for what others thought of him when he learned how to do this. Instead, he focused more on how he felt about himself.

Today Tobias wants to encourage you to look for a psychologist if you suffer from social anxiety, as they have many strategies that can help you overcome SAD. He now wants to teach other people what he has learned on his healing journey. His mission involves letting socially anxious people know that social anxiety is not a sentence for life and that you too can overcome it if you work hard (Atkins, 2016).

The section above provides an encouraging testimonial that shows you that you too can overcome social anxiety. This chapter will focus on other strategies that you can use to overcome social anxiety. I will be specifically talking about exposure and exposure-based therapy, which is a very effective way to treat and overcome social anxiety.

Facing Your Fears

Everyone wants to avoid anxiety-inducing situations, and this is especially the case for people that suffer from social anxiety. When you avoid social situations that you are scared of you may decrease your short-term anxiety, but this avoidance actually increases your anxiety in the long run. This is because avoidance does not let you see that what you expect is not likely to happen or that it won't be as bad as you thought it would be. This is why facing the situations that you avoid is very important. When you face these situations what you are actually doing is establishing self-confidence and decreasing your distress in the long term.

Fear Ladders

In Chapter 3, I already mentioned listing your fears and ranking their intensity as a part of systematic desensitization, so you should look back at this list. This list is also known as a fear ladder, and it has a scale from 0 (which is no social anxiety) to 10 (which is extreme social anxiety). If you have a CBT therapist, you can perform the gradual exposure with them that I mentioned in Chapter 3. If you do not have access to a CBT therapist for whatever reason, you can still face your fears through gradual exposure with the help of this book.

When looking at your list keep in mind that you can have many different situations that invoke social anxiety, so you may want to group similar social situations together. For example, you can have social anxiety towards public speaking and singing in front of an audience, which can all be put under a performing social anxiety group. You can also make lists for different social anxiety themes.

After identifying a certain social situation that makes you socially anxious you can list the steps that are involved in that situation. For example, if you get social anxiety from asking a question during class, you can list the steps in this action (raising your hand, waiting for your teacher to call on you, and asking your question). You may want to make separate fear ladders for each social anxiety theme if you have a lot of different socially anxiety-inducing situations listed.

Your ladder needs to have a variety of different social situations. The ladder ought to have some steps that you are able to accomplish with mild anxiety, some that you can accomplish with moderate anxiety (or an anxiety level that is between small and very large), and the steps that you believe are too anxiety-inducing for you to fulfill. This is because as I already said in Chapter 3, exposure needs to be taken in gradual small steps.

It may be challenging to think of steps on a fear ladder that induce moderate anxiety, which is why you may want to think of other components that can make those steps easier or more difficult. Some examples of these components are:

How long the social situation is -

For instance, you will probably face more anxiety if you deliver an hour-long speech than if you deliver a five-minute one.

Your environment -

For instance, you may feel more anxious if you are talking in a public space rather than in a private one.

What time it is -

For instance, you may feel more socially anxious about asking a question just before your class ends as opposed to asking that question during the beginning of the class when your teacher has more time.

Who you are with -

For instance, your social anxiety may be lower when you are talking to a close friend and higher when you are talking to a stranger.

Exposure

After you have made your list, you can engage in the social situation that induces the least social anxiety and is the least draining. You should do this after having first role-played and imagined this scenario. You can picture yourself in the social situation and imagine what that is like, and you may also role-play what it would be like with a therapist, friend, or family member. After doing this you should engage in this social situation repeatedly until your social anxiety starts to decrease.

If the social situation is one that can last for a longer period of time (such as a party), you will want to remain there until you begin to feel less anxious. If it is a social situation that is shorter, (such as delivering a five-minute speech) you may want to loop it by doing it over and over again for a certain amount of times. Your social anxiety will decrease if you stay in the feared social situation for enough time or if you keep yourself engrossed in that social situation. This is due to the fact that anxiety is very

CHAPTER 6: HOW TO OVERCOME SOCIAL ANXIETY   99

energy-consuming and so it will run out of fuel at some point. You will get more used to that social situation if you continue to face it and you will feel less social anxiety when you do encounter that situation again.

You may want to track your social anxiety level while you are practicing exposure and aim to stay in those social situations until your anxiety/fear level is halved. For example, if you rate talking to an acquaintance as a 6/10 on the fear ladder (with 0 being no social anxiety and 10 being extreme social anxiety) then you may want to keep talking to that acquaintance until your social anxiety level drops to a 3/10). You should also plan exposure exercises well ahead of time so that you feel like what is happening is more manageable. When you plan ahead you should identify the social situation and when you are going to carry it out.

Tracking your progress is important so that you know how the exposure practices are going. You can track what your original social anxiety level is and see how it decreases with each exposure. You can move on to the next social situation on your fear ladder once you can be a part of the social situation several times and experience little to no anxiety.

It is imperative that you do not rush yourself, especially considering how social situations can be very frightening for you. Take all the time you need and be patient with yourself. Remember that you should go at a manageable pace that is not too fast and that you can always pull out of a social situation if enough time has passed, and your anxiety is still extreme. You should make sure to prioritize your mental health during exposure practices by remembering not to overdo yourself or push yourself too far.

Practice, Practice, Practice!

You need to regularly practice in order for exposure to be effective. Certain social situations can be practiced every day (such as greeting the bus driver, for instance), and other social situations should only be done every so often (for instance, going to a party or a social gathering). Do keep in mind though that your social anxiety will go away more rapidly if you practice more often.

You should keep doing exposure practices every once in a while, even after you become comfortable with those social scenarios since it is important to maintain any gains that you earn. For instance, if you have gotten over your social anxiety in study groups you should still go to study groups every couple of months so that your social anxiety towards that social situation does not return. You will also want to re-rate your fear ladders every so often so that you know what your progress looks like and so you are aware of the social situations and steps that still need to be worked on. Also, experiencing social anxiety is normal when you face social situations that you are afraid of, so try to remember that.

Recompense Your Bravery

Facing social situations that scare you is certainly not easy, which is why you should give yourself rewards when you expose yourself to these situations. You can use rewards to motivate yourself to work towards your goals. For instance, you can treat yourself to some ice cream, watch your favorite movie, order your favorite item at your school's cafeteria, or buy an item you have been wanting for yourself for a while once you feel little to no anxiety during exposure. You should also motivate yourself through positive and friendly self-talk (such as saying, "I was able to do it!").

What if My Social Anxiety Comes Back?

Lastly, do not give up if you realize that your social anxiety comes back. This can take place every once in a while, and it can especially happen when you are very stressed or when you are transitioning from one thing to another (such as switching schools). This is a normal occurrence and all it means is that you should engage in exposure again with the tools that you have learned so far. It is important for you to remember that managing social anxiety is a process that can last for all of your life (Anxiety Canada, n.d.).

Mastering the Art of Conversation

The first step in mastering the art of conversation is choosing where you will be having that conversation. You will want to choose a place that interests and stimulates you and the person(s) you will be talking with. This works because you will seem more interesting to the other person if you are in an interesting and exciting place. That place will make them feel good, but they will not be able to exactly identify what is making them feel good. Therefore, they may think that what is making them feel good is what is in front of them, which is you and your words.

Then you will want to prepare for that conversation through your own self-talk. For instance, tell yourself that you will be present as your best self during that conversation. In order to do this, you can remind yourself of a time in which you were meeting with someone and had a great time. When you remember this, you can ask yourself why that meeting went so well and what happened to make it so successful. You can also ask yourself about the characteristics that distinguish you from others and think about how those traits make you a good person. Thinking about your accomplishments can also help you present as your best self while you are preparing.

You can use small talk if you want, but another suggestion is to be creative and help the person you are talking with to become more positive. For instance, if you are out with your buddies you may start by talking about some good news that your school just came out with. You can also ask others for advice since doing so can make others like you more. The science behind this indicates that you should ask for advice for something that is hard and not easy since if you ask for easy advice people may view you as fake or incompetent. Also, make sure that you are only obtaining advice from the person you asked it from. Doing this will prevent you from being seen as desperate by other people.

While your conversation carries out you will also want to compliment people in an honest manner. Compliments that are not sincere will probably not get a good response, which is why I emphasize the "honest" part. You may also want to ask a question before the meeting ends. This question should get others to talk about themselves. You can ask them questions about their hobbies or what they enjoy doing. You may also ask them for book, podcast, or blog recommendations. However, do make sure that these questions are asked in a manner that is appropriate to the conversation context instead of asking those questions out of nowhere (Psychology Compass, 2017).

Here are some other tips that can help you master the art of conversation:

- Avoid too many details and get to your point

- Assume you will not understand the person you are talking with, so you are curious about them

- Be less formal when socializing

- Foster enthusiasm when you talk to others

- Hint about your interests

- Make the people around you laugh a little

- Rehearse and prepare before talking to others (Alton, 2017)

Setting Realistic Goals

If you have a mental health practitioner, they will make a plan of treatment for you and you can set your goals based on their recommendations. The treatment goals for Social Anxiety Disorder are usually:

- becoming more confident in social situations that trigger your social anxiety

- changing the negative cognitions that underlie your social anxiety (as you saw in Chapter 3 with CBT)

- giving you better and healthier coping mechanisms (Fritscher, 2020)

However, keep in mind that social anxiety treatment is not an overnight thing and that accomplishing these goals can take time, effort, and energy. This is not said to discourage you, but rather to open your eyes to the reality of what you can expect as someone with SAD. You can start on the road to recovery by making small goals for yourself, and you can aim to increase your confidence by taking small steps that boost it.

For example, let's say that you are self-conscious and socially anxious about talking with a friend at the mall. You can set a realistic goal of meeting with that friend but finding a place that is more quiet and secluded and less busy so that you do not push yourself too far. You would want to do this because you may feel overwhelmed and socially anxious if you and your friend are in a big mall with lots of people and activities in it, which is why you could pick a more private space.

You can begin to boost their confidence by first imagining what it would be like to meet up with your friend outside of your home. After imagining this, you could also role-play this scenario with a therapist or with family members as well. Then you would be ready to finally meet up with that friend in that certain private space.

You would follow the rules of exposure that I just outlined and try to make this meeting happen every so often (for example, once a week) so you can practice. Once your social anxiety has gone down enough to the point in which it is minimal or non-existent you can try moving to a place that is busier. Again, once you are comfortable and less anxious in that busier place you can finally move on to your final goal of meeting with that friend at a mall. You can use this example with any other kind of social goals you may have. The key is to remember to be realistic by gradually exposing yourself and going at the pace that is right for you.

Key Takeaways

- Facing the things you avoid is critical since when you confront these events, what you're really doing is boosting your self-confidence and decreasing your discomfort in the long run.

- If you want to make strides in social anxiety, learn how to have great conversations. When you can do this well, it'll be easier for you to find friends and enjoy being in social situations more.

- The aims of social anxiety therapy are generally to become more confident in social situations that cause your social anxiety, modify negative beliefs that underlie your social anxiety, and give you better and healthier coping strategies.

- Treatment for social anxiety is not a quick process, and attaining these objectives will take time, effort, and energy.

Chapter 7

How to Boost Your Teen Confidence in Today's World

What would your life be like if you were more confident? What would you be like if you were able to shake off self-doubt and be the best version of yourself? The possibilities are endless. You might find that having more confidence in yourself opens new doors and new opportunities for you.

For instance, you may actually try out for that extracurricular activity if you have more confidence. Let's say you have always wanted to try out for the fencing team at your school, but perhaps you have been too insecure and self-conscious to do so. With a higher level of self-confidence, you may find yourself willing to try out for the fencing team. Whether you actually make the team or not is irrelevant, but for the sake of this thought exercise let's envision that you actually make the team. Joining the fencing team in turn would pave the way for you to make new friends that share the same common interest in fencing. Making these new friends would boost your happiness and decrease your stress levels. As time progresses you may find that you are rather skilled at fencing, and this could open new opportunities for you. You may find yourself applying for colleges that have fencing programs that you are interested in, and college recruiters may even become interested in your fencing skills. This could lead to you possibly getting a sports scholarship because of your fencing.

Having high levels of self-confidence would not just open college opportunities for you. If you have more confidence in yourself, you are more likely to try and seek new friends. You may feel empowered to ask that group of nice students if you can sit with them at lunch, and this can lead to the formation of a new friend group. Your high levels of self-confidence may also encourage you to talk to your chemistry lab partner and ask them to hang out after school. If they say yes, this would result in a new and exciting friendship. But if they reject you your self-confidence would cushion the blow and would not allow it to prevent you from seeking new friendship opportunities. If you were more confident you may also be motivated to ask out your crush on a date (if you are crushing on anyone). This may lead to a budding teenage romance that you will remember when you look back on your teenage years.

Being more confident can also inspire you to pursue your passions and talents. You may find that you are more likely to focus on your talents and put effort into them if you have a higher level of self-confidence. For instance, let's say that you have artistic talent and that art is one of your passions, and that your school is hosting an art contest. With a lower self-confidence, you may find yourself discouraged from participating in the art contest, but this would not be so with a higher level of self-confidence. If you are confident in yourself and in the art, you make you will be more likely to take the risk of entering the competition. You may also be more likely to devote more time to your artwork, which may lead to your art teacher recognizing your talent. In the long run, your dedication to your art may even land you a spot at an art school if that is what you wish to do for your career.

The following scenarios above are just some of the many outcomes that you can obtain if you become more confident in yourself. This chapter will focus on how to boost your self-confidence so that you can radically and positively transform your life into the life that you want. Keep on reading to learn more about how you can achieve this.

Shaking Off Self-Doubt

If you're plagued by self-doubt, it's time to take action and build confidence in yourself. You can start by seeking out opportunities and embracing positive feedback from others. Being confident prepares you for the experiences you will encounter in your life. When you are confident you don't back away and instead progress towards opportunities and individuals. Having a high level of self-confidence also helps you to keep trying even if things do not turn out how you wanted them to. However, having a low level of self-confidence decreases the chances that you will approach people that are new to you and makes you less likely to try out new things. People with low self-confidence are unlikely to keep trying if they do not succeed the first time. Therefore, having low self-confidence can prevent you from unlocking your true potential.

Also, know that confidence can increase and decrease for every single human being out there. Some of the most confident people you see out there may have days in which they have a lower sense of self-esteem. Make sure to be kind and understanding towards yourself if your confidence is shaken. Do not be harsh on yourself and instead think about what caused this, and how you could have behaved in a different way, and keep this in mind for the future. You can talk about this with a close friend or family member that cares for you. You can later remember all of your accomplishments and strengths so that you can return to the game.

Adolescence is a time filled with a lack of self-confidence, for even children with high levels of confidence can have a hard time maintaining their levels when they grow into their teenage years. Being a teenager may often involve insecurities, self-doubts, and a shifting body image. However, you can absolutely increase your self-confidence. Improving your self-confidence can help you make great choices, deal with pressure from your peers, work through hard romantic relationships, and get back on track after a setback (Morin, 2021). The following sections include some ways you can shake off self-doubt and increase your self-confidence:

Believe in Your Abilities

Allow yourself to take on chores and other activities on your own, especially if your parents let you do something without them helping you. You can believe in your abilities by doing things such as taking care of your siblings if you have any, learning how to cook on your own through Youtube videos, or learning a new skill such as painting on your own. This will help you believe in your capabilities (Gordon, 2022). When you doubt your abilities, you can feel unprepared, less than, or unworthy, and this in turn may lead you to avoid circumstances and individuals that you might have fun with and grow with. Thus, you need to believe in your abilities. You probably have heard of the phrase, "If you believe, you can achieve!" This is a phrase that you should always think of.

You may have been told before that you are intelligent, kind, a bright student, a great athlete, or an excellent writer. Hearing praise like this about your abilities and skills can increase your confidence in yourself, but this will only happen if you agree with the praise and believe you have these positive qualities. Not having a good sense of self-confidence can mean that you may doubt when people make these compliments to you. You need to feel like you are competent and able in order to really be confident in yourself. One way you can do this is by working on your talents and skills. Practice and learning make perfect, and practicing and learning what you are already skilled in can make you believe you are capable. Being confident will help you identify your abilities and further develop them. Your confidence will be boosted when you discover these capabilities and become proud of what you have achieved.

Create a Confident Mindset

Your inner voice may tell you things such as "I can't do this," but you can create a confident mindset by telling yourself, "I can do this." Reassure yourself that you are able to achieve your goals instead of putting yourself down. You can do this by reminding yourself of any challenges you have overcome before and by coming up with affirmations. An affirmation is a statement that you will think of whenever you feel self-conscious or insecure. An example of an affirmation you can tell yourself is, "I am capable of doing this and more."

Give Yourself Permission to Make Errors

Try to take risks as long as they are within reason. For example, a reasonable risk would be trying out for your school's choir, and an unreasonable risk would be using drugs and alcohol You can take risks such as volunteering at a project or a fundraising event, joining a committee at school, raising your hand in class whenever you have a question or feel like you know the answer to a teacher's question, or talking to your crush during a class that you two have in common. Do not shelter yourself or expect your parents to get you out of every single setback you have. Let yourself deal with disappointment without feeling like you have failed, and instead, teach yourself how to learn from what happened and keep moving forward. This will make you more resilient (Gordon, 2022).

Go Outside of Your Comfort Zone

Do something that you want to do but you feel like you would need more confidence to do it. For instance, you may want to sign up for the talent show at your school, but you may feel like you don't have the confidence to do so. Instead of repressing your wish to perform at the talent show you could sign up for it and see how it goes. Doing this will increase your self-confidence and show you that it is okay to try out new things even if they are outside of your comfort zone. Push yourself and go for it! Once you have fulfilled that item that is outside of your comfort zone you may choose another thing you can try out. You can keep completing this process, for your confidence will increase with every step you take.

Make Your Talents Shine

Don't let your weaknesses get in the way of you doing things that you are good at. This may feel contradictory since people are often encouraged to put in a lot of effort to get better at their weaknesses. This may be worth doing if it involves something important, like improving your grade at a school subject you are not particularly good at. However, you should not only be focusing on your weaknesses. Make sure to devote time to what you are good at as well.

Do Your Homework

I encourage you to work on your assignments, study and get ready for your classes, quizzes, and tests. This may feel like an elaborate plot to get you to finally listen to your parents and work on that math homework you have been dreading, but I promise you it is not. I say this because if you stay on top of your homework, you will have more confidence when the tests and finals roll around. By steadily doing your schoolwork you will be able to defend yourself against academic stress and test anxiety. After all, you are going to be less nervous before a big test if you have studied for it.

Dare to Be Who You Really Are

Let everyone see you as you really are without feeling like you have to hide anything. This includes being transparent with your insecurities and errors. You are more likely to be able to overcome your insecurities if you do not feel like you have to conceal them. Cherish your quirks and stop trying to be like another person that is not like you. Being who you really are is something that requires a lot of confidence and bravery from you. However, you will be more confident in yourself if you act as who you really are. This confidence will in turn increase your self-esteem (KidsHealth, n.d).

Activities You Can Do to Build Confidence

- Draw yourself

- Start a positive thinking journal

- Also make a gratitude journal

- Think about your self-esteem as the week progresses

- Give advice to another kid that has a hard time with their self-esteem

- Help increase the self-esteem of a fictional character

- Focus on areas you can make positive changes in

- Jot down what your positive characteristics are

- Exercise and do physical activity

Boosting the Self-Esteem

Boosting your self-esteem is not just crucial for your mental health, it is also essential in order to prevent bullying. Bullies usually target teenagers that are not as confident in themselves, which is why building your self-esteem will not only help you deal with bullying but also drive the bullies away. Here are some ways in which you can improve your self-esteem:

Encourage Your Self-Improvement

You may feel like you have failed if you have a hard time with a certain skill. For example, you may feel dumb if you struggle with a school subject like math. You may also feel like you will never be good at singing if you do not make it into the choir. In order to have good self-esteem you need to balance your self-improvement and your self-acceptance. You can accept your flaws and simultaneously try to improve on your shortcomings. Look for help instead of telling yourself that you are dumb just because you are not good at something.

Identify your weak points but also acknowledge your strengths. Once you do this you can set goals for yourself and problem-solve with the problem-solving model that I showed you so that you can improve in the things that you have a hard time with. Set goals that you can achieve and that you can control. Then you can plan how you will obtain these goals.

Praise Your Effort and Not Your Outcome

Instead of telling yourself things such as, "I got an A+ on that test!" you can tell yourself, "I did a great job at studying for that test!" Or instead of telling yourself, "I did a good job at helping us win that game," you can think, "I practiced a lot for that game, and it paid off." Show yourself that not succeeding every single time is okay and that what really matters is how hard you try. You cannot always control how things turn out, but you can always control how hard you try. This is why you should praise your hard work and energy so that you do not feel like your worth depends on your success.

Work on Your Self-Worth

Your self-worth is a part of your self-esteem, and it is something that you need to work on. You will have a hard time being confident when circumstances aren't tailored to your needs if you only feel worthy when you weigh a specific amount or get a specific number of likes on social media. This is why you should not base your self-worth on others, on superficial items, or on external situations since this will decrease your confidence over time. Instead, highlight what you value and what you believe in and live by that. Basing your self-worth on your values and how you live according to these values will build a strong self-worth foundation. Place more value on being a good person rather than on being conventionally attractive or skinny.

Compliment Your Character

Character traits you may have such as leadership, empathy, generosity, cooperation, courage, and taking responsibility should not go unrecognized and you should praise yourself for them. You may only compliment yourself when you accomplish something in school or in sports, but you should also compliment your positive traits. You should still praise the hard work that you put into sports and school, but these things are not lifelong qualities like your character. Therefore, you should focus on what makes you a good human being.

Give Yourself Positive Self-Talk

The way in which you talk to yourself will largely influence how you feel about yourself. For example, telling yourself things like, "Everyone dislikes me" or "I'm very ugly" is obviously going to make you feel bad. This is why you should talk to yourself in a way that is healthy. You can do this by realizing that these thoughts are false and acknowledging that they can be harmful to you. Learn how to re-evaluate thoughts such as "I'm so dumb that I'm going to fail math class," and instead re-evaluate them in a more realistic light such as, "I will pass this class if I put a lot of effort into it."

Spend Time With Your Family

Spending time with your family can make you feel important in their lives and that helps with your self-esteem. The time you spend with them can also form a relationship that is more solid. Having a good relationship with your family becomes crucial as you encounter more difficulties. After all, you will have an easier time if you know that your family loves you.

Do Not Compare Yourself to Others

Value your individuality and gifts instead of comparing yourself with your siblings, your friends, or other acquaintances. You may label one of your siblings as "the smart one" or "the pretty one." However, comparing yourself with your siblings can lead to you envying them or even teasing them. Comparing yourself to others can also negatively impact how you see yourself, which is why you should avoid this (Gordon 2022).

Building the Best Version of Yourself

You can begin to build the best version of yourself by encouraging yourself to seek new opportunities. Try out different activities, challenge yourself, and discover any talents you may have. Another part of being the best version of yourself is finding equilibrium between your freedom and your parent's guidance. This will be easier to do if your parents give you the chance to go through the consequences of your actions and learn from your errors. This will make you have a heightened sense of confidence and will help you make better decisions. This may be harder if you have stricter parents, but you may find that they will give you more leeway and freedom if you are obedient and diligent.

You can build the best version of yourself by going after your passions. Doing activities that you enjoy will increase your confidence and spread it into all of your life's other aspects. Another way to do this is to love yourself unconditionally. It may be hard, but you can try to wake up every day and say that you love yourself just how you are. Know that it is okay to be imperfect as all humans are, and that what matters is how hard you work and how much effort you put in.

Volunteering can be a rewarding experience and it will also help you be more grateful for your life. Volunteering also fosters compassion in you towards those that are in a worse position than you. You can also set life goals for yourself just like you can set goals to overcome your social anxiety. However, make sure that these goals are reasonable since your self-confidence can suffer if you try to go after something that cannot be achieved (Gordon, 2022).

Key Takeaways

- If self-doubt is your downfall, take action to build confidence by seeking opportunities and surrounding yourself with positive feedback.

- Maintaining high self-esteem does wonders for your mental health, and it can even keep you safe from bullies.

-

Pushing yourself to explore different opportunities is how you start becoming the best version of yourself.

- Trying new things, learning as much as you can, and uncovering any hidden talents are all part of this process.

Conclusion

This book aimed to convey a message that stressed the importance of overcoming your social anxiety and developing better social skills. I have covered a wide variety of topics in this book, which I will summarize in the following sections below.

Social Anxiety Disorder is a Mental Health Condition

Social Anxiety Disorder is listed as a mental health disorder in the Diagnostic and Statistical Manual of Mental Health Disorders. This is a mental health condition that makes people like you strongly fear being judged, embarrassed, rejected, or scrutinized. This disorder has several negative implications for the people that have it, including deteriorating personal relationships. However, it is a treatable condition that has a variety of treatment plans. CBT and DBT are some of the most known types of treatments for social anxiety, and antidepressants are also used for this mental health condition.

Signs of Social Anxiety

One key sign that is always present in social anxiety is having anxiety or fear towards one or multiple social situations. This social situation should almost always provoke anxiety or fear in the patient, and this fear is out of proportion to the actual situation that is taking place. The distress that is caused by social anxiety has to be significant and needs to deteriorate the patient's functioning. Some signs of social anxiety include struggling to make friends, being scared of embarrassment, having a hard time when beginning a conversation, dreading future social circumstances, or having anxiety before a social event starts.

Social Skills Are Extremely Important

Social skills are manners in which people communicate with others and behaviors that everyone needs to begin a relationship with another person. These skills are also needed if you want to keep older relationships, which is why they are extremely critical. Social skills have proved to be important since they predict how successful a person will be in the future. For instance, they can predict whether someone will graduate from college or not. Having good social skills also increases your independence, success, and well-being in the workplace. Social skills are also very important because they allow you to be more successful in certain situations and increase how confident you are in your abilities. They also prepare you for better social interactions in the future and thus prepare you for adulthood. You should always check for social skill problems you may have since these issues may negatively impact your interactions with others, your ability to find a job and thrive, and how well you do in school.

CBT is an Effective Treatment for Social Anxiety

Cognitive Behavioral Therapy (CBT) is a strong evidence-based therapy that has been proven to be 50—75% effective in treating anxiety and depression. A central concept of CBT is that thoughts, behaviors, and feelings all influence each other. Your thoughts affect how you behave and feel, and your behavior affects how you think and feel. Your feelings also affect how you think and behave. In CBT there are many different treatment goals for people with social anxiety, but one of the most common ones involves changing mistaken beliefs that make patients think that other people are judging them.

There are two components in CBT, and these are the cognitive and behavioral components. The cognitive component involves changing the thoughts that underlie the patient's problematic thoughts. Cognitive restructuring is a cognitive technique that does this. To do this technique you have to identify your distorted thoughts and compare them to what is actually happening. You can do this by asking yourself if there is any evidence that backs up your socially anxious thoughts.

The behavioral component of CBT involves systematic desensitization. Systematic desensitization involves gradually exposing the patient to what they fear, and in your case that would be social situations. The three steps in systematic desensitization involve relaxation strategies, listing and ranking your fears, and exposing yourself to what incites anxiety and fear. This process has to be done very gradually since it can actually worsen your anxiety if it is rushed. Performing behavioral experiments (such as experimenting by going to a party or another social gathering) is another behavioral technique.

DBT is an Effective Treatment for Social Anxiety

Dialectical Behavioral Therapy (DBT) has been proven to be more effective than other treatments when it comes to treating social anxiety. DBT is meant to help people that struggle with emotional regulation and have tendencies that are self-destructive. DBT can be provided in an individual therapy, over the phone, or in group therapy. When used in individual therapy, DBT helps integrate skills into your life that allow you to function in your reality, and it also establishes coping mechanisms that you can use during stressful circumstances.

Mindfulness is one aspect of DBT that helps ground you in the present moment. This helps people with social anxiety since these individuals heavily focus on their social performance, and mindfulness shatters the cycle of self-focused attention. Another skill that you can learn from DBT is interpersonal effectiveness. You can practice interpersonal effectiveness by remembering the acronym GIVE. The G stands for gentle, which means that you should not threaten, judge, or attack others. The I stand for interest, so you show that you are interested in that other person by listening to them and being present with them. The V stands for validate, so you would acknowledge how the other person thinks and feels. The E stands for easy since you want to have an easy-going attitude.

Distress tolerance is another type of DBT skill that you can practice by doing radical acceptance, or accepting your reality. You can also practice this skill through self-soothing coping skills such as spending time with your pets. Emotional regulation is another DBT skill that you can practice by acting opposite to your emotions.

Strengthening Your Social Skills

You can strengthen your social skills by actively listening. In order to actively listen to others, you must pay attention while you listen, paraphrase what they said, avoid judging the other person, ask questions, and be patient. Ignoring people that constantly hurt you is another social skill that you can fulfill by avoiding that person without being rude to them.

You can learn how to join conversations by choosing a group, listening to what is being said, making questions, showing interest, and talking about yourself. To share information, you should first make sure you want to talk about what you are going to share, make sure that the situation is appropriate, inoculate people by starting with a little bit of information and make sure you can trust the person you are talking with. Another way to strengthen your social skills involves the empathic process, in which you do not use private information against the other person, try to accept the other person as they are, and give yourself a "time in" in which you can self-soothe.

Exposure is a Key Component to Overcoming Social Anxiety

A great way to overcome social anxiety is by exposing yourself to the social situations you fear. You can do this by listing and ranking your fears. Then you can list the steps that are involved in every single fear. You can begin exposing yourself to the social situation by imagining yourself in it or by role-playing it. Once you have done that you can actually start engaging in that social situation until your social anxiety is little to none.

Boost Your Self-Confidence and Self-Esteem

You can boost your self-confidence by believing in your abilities and therefore doing things on your own. You can also increase your self-confidence by having a confident mindset in which you tell yourself things such as, "I can do it!" Allowing yourself to mess up is another way you can do this. Taking risks (such as trying out for a sport or an extracurricular) is a way in which you can give yourself permission to make mistakes. Going out of your comfort zone and working on your talents are other ways in which you can boost your self-confidence.

You can also boost your self-esteem by encouraging yourself to improve in areas that are not your strengths. Praising your hard work instead of your results is another way to increase your self-esteem. Try not to base your self-worth on external events, superficial items, or other people since doing so can harm your self-esteem. Talk positively to yourself and compliment your positive character traits. Also, try to spend time with your family without comparing yourself to your siblings or any other person.

This book has fulfilled its promise of significantly improving your life by assisting you in defeating social anxiety and by teaching you how to strengthen your social skills. I have done this by giving you helpful information and strategies that can help you in your healing journey. This book has also achieved this by encouraging you to seek psychological help from a mental health practitioner. Thus, I also provided the solution to increased social anxiety levels in your age group by giving you the tools and resources that you need in order to cope with social anxiety.

One thing that I want you to take away from this book is that social anxiety and underdeveloped social skills are things that you can overcome. This book wants to serve as a beacon of hope for all socially anxious teenagers by showing you that recovery from SAD is indeed possible. You can also develop social skills by practicing them and following the tips and advice that you have acquired by reading this book. So go on, take all the wisdom you have learned from this book and use it to live your best teenage life!

Leaving a Review

As a self-published author, I find it important not only to write great books but also provide my readers with the best value possible. Being an Indie writer means I don't have access to all the perks of a traditional publisher, such as a publicist to get the word out about my latest releases. That's where you come in. A little bit of your time can go a long way towards helping me spread the word and I would be most appreciative if you would consider posting your honest thoughts about this book on Amazon.

Your review remains one of the most valuable promotional tools available. Reviews are vital in helping new readers find books they will enjoy reading. So if you've enjoyed this book, please consider leaving an honest rating or review by going to this book's page on Amazon. Good ratings and reviews from readers can help me attract new readers who will also enjoy my writing.

Thank you for your support,

Grace

About the Author

Grace is a well-known parenting author who has written several books on the topic. She has dedicated her life to assisting families through her writings. Her greatest enjoyment in life is being a mother because it's the most gratifying job she's ever had. She likes to write books that touch on all the different aspects of parenting and personal experiences, such as her encounters with her children.

Her love for writing began when she discovered a parenting technique for her explosive son, who was diagnosed with ADHD and ODD, that outperformed others. She was determined to get the word out to other parents as soon as possible. With time, this has developed into something bigger where she is able to share great pieces of advice that can truly change lives.

She also incorporates insights from other parents to offer an enlightening reading experience for all of her readers. Grace hopes that families will be inspired to change the way they think and make better parenting decisions by reading her books.

She enjoys reading novels and watching movies with her family on the weekends.

Visit her profile on Amazon to learn more about her other works - **https://www.amazon.com/author/gracecohen**

References

Alton, L. (2017, April 12). *6 Tips to Rule the Art of Conversation.* SUCCESS. https://www.success.com/6-tips-to-rule-the-art-of-conversation/

American Psychological Association. (2017, July). *What Is Cognitive Behavioral Therapy?* American Psychological Association. https://www.apa.org/ptsd-guideline/patients-and-families/cognitive-behavioral

Ankrom, S. (2020, December 27). *Systematic Desensitization for Panic Disorders.* Verywell Mind. https://www.verywellmind.com/systematic-desensitization-2584

Anwar, B. (2022, April 27). *4 DBT Therapy Techniques.* Talkspace. https://www.talkspace.com/blog/dbt-therapy-techniques/

Anwar, B. (2022, May 25). *Radical Acceptance: Definition & How It Can Help.* Talkspace. https://www.talkspace.com/blog/radical-acceptance/

Anxiety Canada. (n.d.-a). *FACING YOUR FEARS: EXPOSURE.* Anxiety Canada. https://www.anxietycanada.com/sites/default/files/FacingFears_ Exposure.pdf

Anxiety Canada. (n.d.-b). *SELF-HELP STRATEGIES FOR SOCIAL ANXIETY.* Anxiety Canada. https://www.anxietycanada.com/sites/default/files/adult_hmsoc ial.pdf

Atkins, T. J. (2016, September 7). *My Lifelong Struggle With Social Anxiety.* ADAA. https://adaa.org/living-with-anxiety/personal-stories/my-lifelong -struggle-social-anxiety

Carmichael, C. (2021, January 15). *When and How to Share Personal Information.* Dr. Chloe; Carmichael Psychology PLLC. https://www.drchloe.com/blog/openup/

Carroll, R. (2016, July 14). *Starved, tortured, forgotten: Genie, the feral child who left a mark on researchers.* The Guardian; Guardian News & Media Limited. https://www.theguardian.com/society/2016/jul/14/genie-feral-c hild-los-angeles-researchers

Cognitive Behavioral Therapy Los Angeles. (n.d.). *How Effective Is Cognitive Behavioral Therapy.* https://cogbtherapy.com/how-effective-is-cbt-compared-to-other -treatments

Cuncic, A. (2020, March 19). *How to Join a Conversation.* Verywell M   i   n   d   . https://www.verywellmind.com/how-to-join-a-conversation-389 4035

Cuncic, A. (2021, September 1). *Therapy for Social Anxiety Disorder.* Verywell Mind; Dotdash Meredith. https://www.verywellmind.com/how-is-cbt-used-to-treat-sad-30 24945

Cuncic, A. (2022, February 13). *Practicing Active Listening in Your Daily Conversations.* Verywell Mind; Dotdash Meredith. https://www.verywellmind.com/what-is-active-listening-302434 3#toc-how-to-practice-active-listening

Davis, J. (2020, February 28). *4 Tips to Effectively Ask for Help—and Get a Yes.* Psychology Today; Sussex Publishers, LLC. https://www.psychologytoday.com/us/blog/tracking-wonder/2 02002/4-tips-effectively-ask-help-and-get-ycs

Debbie. (2012, July 17). *6 Ways To Get The MOST out of DBT (Dialectical Behavior Therapy).* Healing from BPD. https://www.my-borderline-personality-disorder.com/2012/07/ 6-ways-to-get-the-most-out-of-dbt-dialectical-behavior-therapy.h tml

Doyle, A. (2020, October 21). *What Are Problem-Solving Skills?* The Balance Careers. https://www.thebalancecareers.com/problem-solving-skills-with-examples-2063764

Fritscher, L. (2020, February 22). *The Goals of Phobia Treatment.* Verywell Mind. https://www.verywellmind.com/goals-of-therapy-2671657#:~:text=The%20goals%20of%20treatment%20for

Gordon, S. (2022, January 13). *13 Ways to Build Self-Esteem and Prevent Bullying.* Verywell Family. https://www.verywellfamily.com/how-building-selfesteem-can-prevent-bullying-460679

Gray-Grant, D. (2021, November 30). *How to become better at following directions.* Publication Coach. https://www.publicationcoach.com/better-at-following-directions/

Gross, G. (2015, January 9). *How to Use the Empathic Process.* Dr. Gail Gross, http://drgailgross.com/use-empathic-process/

Gross, G. (2015, October 16). *Conflict Resolution for Tweens and Teens.* HuffPost. https://www.huffpost.com/entry/conflict-resolution-for-tweens-and-teens_b_8286108

Guy-Evans, O. (2022, March 30). *Social Anxiety in Teens: Signs, Symptoms, and How to Help.* Www.simplypsychology.org. https://www.simplypsychology.org/social-anxiety-in-teens.html

Harned, M. S., & Botanov, Y. (2016). Dialectical Behavior Therapy Skills Training Is Effective Intervention. *Psychiatric Times,* *33*(3). https://www.psychiatrictimes.com/view/dialectical-behavior-therapy-skills-training-effective-intervention

Healthy@UH. (2020, April 24). *8 Soothing Techniques to Help Relieve Anxiety.* University Hospitals. https://www.uhhospitals.org/Healthy-at-UH/articles/2020/04/8-soothing-techniques-to-help-relieve-anxiety

Hires, C. (2019, October 25). *Using DBT Skills to Reduce Social Anxiety.* Specialized Therapy. https://www.specializedtherapy.com/using-dbt-skills-to-reduce-social-anxiety/

Hofmann, S. G., Asnaani, A., Vonk, I. J. J., Sawyer, A. T., & Fang, A. (2012). The Efficacy of Cognitive Behavioral Therapy: A Review of Meta-Analyses. *Cognitive Therapy and Research, 36*(5), 427–440. https://doi.org/10.1007/s10608-012-9476-1

Indeed Editorial Team. (2019, December 12). *13 Ways To Start a Conversation (With Examples).* Indeed. https://www.indeed.com/career-advice/career-development/how-to-start-a-conversation

Intrepid Mental Wellness, PLLC. (n.d.). *3 Quick DBT Skills to Help Regulate Anxiety That Anyone Can Use!* Intrepid Mental Wellness, PLLC: Psychiatric Nurse Practitioners. Intrepid Mental Health .

https://www.intrepidmentalhealth.com/blog/3-quick-dbt-skills-to-help-regulate-anxiety-that-anyone-can-use

Jefferies, P., & Ungar, M. (2020). Social anxiety in young people: A prevalence study in seven countries. *PLOS ONE, 15*(9), e0239133. https://doi.org/10.1371/journal.pone.0239133

Kashtan, I., & Kashtan, M. (n.d.). *Basics of Nonviolent Communication.* Bay NVC. https://baynvc.org/basics-of-nonviolent-communication/

Kelly, B. (2021, July 28). *10 Tips How To Develop Interpersonal Skills»* Peep Strategy. Peep Strategy. https://peepstrategy.com/how-to-develop-interpersonal-skills/

Kelly, B. (2021, July 30). *Non-verbal Communication: Why It Matters, How To Do It Well.* Peep Strategy. https://peepstrategy.com/non-verbal-communication/

Kelly, B. (2021, August 5). *Effective Verbal Communication -How Can You Use It?* Peep Strategy. https://peepstrategy.com/effective-verbal-communication/

KidsHealth. (n.d.). *Confidence.* The Nemours Foundation. https://kidshealth.org/en/teens/confidence.html

KidsHealth. (2019, February). *Sportsmanship.* The Nemours Foundation. https://kidshealth.org/en/teens/sportsmanship.html

KidsHealth. (2022, August). *Apologizing.* KidsHealth. The Nemours Foundation. https://kidshealth.org/en/teens/apologies.html

Lake, M. (2018, January 2). *The Importance of Social Skills: Raising a Socially Intelligent Child.* GoodTherapy. https://www.goodtherapy.org/blog/importance-of-social-skills-r aising-socially-intelligent-child-0102184

Lindholm, H., Morrison, I., Krettek, A., Malm, D., Novembre, G., & Handlin, L. (2020). Genetic risk-factors for anxiety in healthy individuals: polymorphisms in genes important for the HPA axis. *BMC Medical Genetics, 21*(1). https://doi.org/10.1186/s12881-020-01123-w

Lozano, D. (2019, July 8). *Teen Social Skills 101: A Guide to Surviving the Most Awkward Time of Your Life.* 24/7 Teach. https://247teach.org/blog/2019/5/23/teen-social-skills-101

Mayo Clinic Staff. (2022, May 13). *Being assertive: Reduce stress, communicate better.* Mayo Clinic; Mayo Foundation for Medical Education and Research. https://www.mayoclinic.org/healthy-lifestyle/stress-management /in-depth/assertive/art-20044644

Morin, A. (2021, February 20). *8 Essential Strategies for Raising a Confident Teen.* Verywell Family. https://www.verywellfamily.com/essential-strategies-for-raising-a -confident-teen-2611002

Morris, L., & Tieperman, J. (2022, August 18). *What Are Some Activities to Build Confidence in Teenagers?* WikiHow. https://www.wikihow.com/What-Are-Some-Activities-to-Build-Confidence-in-Teenagers

National Collaborating Centre for Mental Health. (2013). *SOCIAL ANXIETY DISORDER.* National Library of Medicine; British Psychological Society. https://www.ncbi.nlm.nih.gov/books/NBK327674/

National Social Anxiety Center. (n.d.-a). *CBT STRATEGIES TO OVERCOME SOCIAL ANXIETY.* National Social Anxiety Center. https://nationalsocialanxietycenter.com/cognitive-behavioral-therapy/social-anxiety-strategies/

National Social Anxiety Center. (n.d.-b). *COGNITIVE-BEHAVIORAL THERAPY FOR SOCIAL ANXIETY.* National Social Anxiety Center. https://nationalsocialanxietycenter.com/cognitive-behavioral-therapy/

Paradigm Treatment. (n.d.). *Teen & Young Adult Social Anxiety Disorder.* Paradigm Treatment; *Paradigm Treatment Centers, LLC.* https://paradigmtreatment.com/anxiety-teens-young-adults/social/

Psychology Compass. (2017, August 23). *Mastering the art of conversation.* Psychology Compass.

https://psychologycompass.com/blog/mastering-the-art-of-conversation/

Pun, J. (2019, September 22). *What is Online Cognitive Behavioral Therapy (CBT)?* Starling Minds. https://www.starlingminds.com/what-is-online-cognitive-behavioral-therapy-cbt-starling-minds/#:~:text=Research%20shows%20that%20CBT%20is

Raypole, C. (2019, February 25). *How Systematic Desensitization Can Help You Overcome Fear.* Healthline. https://www.healthline.com/health/systematic-desensitization#how-it-works

Raypole, C. (2021, September 16). *How CBT Can Help You Manage Social Anxiety Symptoms.* Healthline; Healthline Media. https://www.healthline.com/health/anxiety/social-anxiety-disorder-cognitive-behavioral-therapy#effectiveness

Russell, L. (2022, March 10). *Social Anxiety in Teenagers: 5 Things You Should Know.* They Are the Future. https://www.theyarethefuture.co.uk/social-anxiety-in-teenager/

Salters-Pedneault, K. (2022, July 22). *How Emotion Regulation Skills Promote Stability.* Verywell Mind. https://www.verywellmind.com/emotion-regulation-skills-training-425374

Sanders, P. (2021, October 25). *9 Tips To Master The Art Of Conversation.* Get the Friends You Want. https://getthefriendsyouwant.com/art-of-conversation/

Schimelpfening, N. (2022, July 22). *What Is Dialectical Behavior Therapy (DBT)?* Verywell Mind. https://www.verywellmind.com/dialectical-behavior-therapy-106 7402

Sharna, K. (2019, October 12). *Importance of Social Skills For Students.* The Asian School. https://www.theasianschool.net/blog/importance-of-social-skills -for-students/

Shortridge Academy. (2020, November 24). *Helping Your Teen Build Social Skills.* Shortridge Academy. https://www.shortridgeacademy.com/helping-your-teen-build-s ocial-skills/

Sirota, M. (2014, August 17). *The Real Difference Between Personal & Professional Relationships.* LinkedIn. https://www.linkedin.com/pulse/20140817051857-76474304-t he-real-difference-between-personal-professional-relationships/

Skills You Need. (n.d.). *What are Social Skills?* https://www.skillsyouneed.com/ips/social-skills.html

Social Communication. (n.d.). *Turn-Taking.* Social Communication. https://socialcommunication.truman.edu/hidden-social-dimensi ons/turn-taking/

Substance Abuse and Mental Health Services Administration. (2016, June). *Table 16, DSM-IV to DSM-5 Social Phobia/Social Anxiety Disorder Comparison.* Nih.gov; Substance Abuse and

Mental Health Services Administration (US). https://www.ncbi.nlm.nih.gov/books/NBK519712/table/ch3.t1 2/

Sudhir, P. M., Math, S. B., & Pinjarkar, R. G. (2015). Brief cognitive behavior therapy in patients with social anxiety disorder: A preliminary investigation. *Indian Journal of Psychological Medicine, 37*(1), 20. https://doi.org/10.4103/0253-7176.150808

United We Care. (2021, August 30). *How to Respectfully Ignore Someone Without Hurting Them.* United We Care. https://www.unitedwecare.com/how-to-ignore-someone/

Voss, P., Thomas, M. E., Cisneros-Franco, J. M., & de Villers-Sidani, É. (2017). Dynamic Brains and the Changing Rules of Neuroplasticity: Implications for Learning and Recovery. *Frontiers in Psychology, 8*(1657). https://doi.org/https://doi.org/10.3389/fpsyg.2017.01657

Printed in Great Britain
by Amazon